I0039158

A History of the Hole Family

in England and America

BY

CHARLES ELMER RICE,

ALLIANCE, OHIO.

1904.

ILLUSTRATED WITH 42 PORTRAITS AND ENGRAVINGS

With Appendices on the Hanna, Grubb, Douglas-Morton, Miller and Morris Families.

THE R. M. SCRANTON PUBLISHING CO., ALLIANCE, OHIO.

CONTENTS.

CHAPTER XII.

CHAPTER XIII.

CHAPTER XIV.

LIST OF ILLUSTRATIONS.

PREFACE.

When the writer of this book visited his relative Dean Hole, at Rochester, England, that very Reverend, learned and witty prelate gave him all possible assistance in compiling the Hole Family History, but informed him that when he (the Dean) was still a young man, at Caunton, he remembered finding his mother's rolls of butter come to the house enveloped in large leaves of vellum, which on closer inspection revealed the dates of birth and baptism of the Dean's ancestors for some hundreds of years back. The Caunton Parish Registers had been thus used for culinary and domestic purposes and the resultant evils and losses would be difficult to determine. Through this butter transaction the Holes probably lost several ancestors. Such an explanation is worth many apologies. In our own country, where records are not well kept, the difficulty of procuring adequate data has been greatly increased by the religious views of those who took literally Paul's advice to "Avoid foolish questions and genealogies, for they are unprofitable and vain." (Titus III., 9.) The writer of the Hole book is obliged to confess that more than once he has been inclined to consign certain members of the family who have persistently neglected to answer letters and interrogatories, to that "Hole in the bottom of the sea," where Mr. McGinty is supposed to have found his place of final sepulture.

The splendid indifference of those who were in a position to give dates and facts will account for many of the gaps and omissions in this volume. In preparing the genealogy of the Hole family, which has been made possible through the generosity of Leonard Hanna Hole, of N. Y., I have been especially helped by and here acknowledge the kindly services of Mr. Henry F. Hole, of Fairbury, Nebraska; Mrs. Annie M. Hobson, of Athens, Ohio; Dean Hole, of Rochester, England, and Judge Warren W. Hole, of Salem, Ohio.

CHAS. ELMER RICE.

Alliance, Ohio, Jan. 1, 1904.

CHAPTER I.

Jacob Hole and Barbara his wife sailed from Plymouth, England, in 1740 and landed after a tedious voyage of many weeks, in Philadelphia.

Just where these founders of the Hole family in America came from has never been known to their descendants. And it was not until the summer of 1900, when the writer was sent to Europe to procure data, search records and write a family history, that we so much as knew their nationality.

It had been a tradition in the family that Jacob Hole was German and came to America from Germany; yet no proof whatever had ever been produced to substantiate the claim or prove the theory. The various intermarriages into the best English families of Pennsylvania and Virginia seemed to indicate that the Holes were of English origin. A thorough search of English records and genealogies has clearly shown that the name is English, though of Norse origin, and a visit to the English branches of the family, to the Estates and Freeholds belonging to them, has enabled the writer to give a tolerably complete and full account of the Holes in England and America. Devonshire, in the south-west of England has been the home of the Hole family for the last one thousand years. The Estate of St. Giles, near Barnstaple, in that county has been owned by HENRY HOLE, until 1835, when the 20*th Henry in succession* died. By the ordinary computation of the length of a generation this would take us to the year 1175, A. D., when the first Henry Hole owned the estate.

Hugh Hole, Barrister, of London, the son of the very Reverend Samuel Reynolds Hole, Dean of Rochester, says, "The first Hole of whom I have any record was my namesake Hugh of Hole, who is recorded in the Annals of the Parish of Lindby is Nottinghamshire, (some few miles from our home of Caunton) as owning land there in the year 1240. In that district, we are direct descendants of the Northmen and I have lived in Norway some 16 years and speak the three Scandinavian dialects. I can still trace, at Caunton, the old Norse language, in many local expressions and can see from the house, on lands owned by our family the old entrenchments made by the Norsemen called to this day, "The Danes Hold or Hall," from which they ruled the land by military law."

The most ancient seat of the Hole family in England, so far as we know, was at Tavistock Abbey, which was finished and dedicated in the year 981. King Ethelred, the Son of Elfrida, confirmed and granted to it "many considerable privileges, making it free from all secular services excepting rates for military expeditions and the repair of bridges and castles."

In the preamble of this instrument he laments that certain persons stained with Infidelity had been allowed without his consent to drive the Monks of Tavistock from their Sacred places and possessions. This "stain of Infidelity," was probably nothing more then a disbelief in the Sanctity of monarchism and the expulsion of the Monks from church benefices, in which they were replaced by the much more deserving secular clergy.

This is the first intimation we have of the early republican views of the Hole family and of their disbelief in the divine rights of Kings: A disbelief which has certainly characterized them throughout their entire history and at last brought them to America. At Tavistock then, the Hole family established themselves and later various members of the family are found at Horse-bridge, at Holesworthy at Exeter and at Hengesdown, (now called Hingston) These names suggest much in favor of the tradition of the Devonshire Holes that they are of Norse origin.

Hengest-dune is not very far from Horse-bridge, and one can not help entertaining the conjecture that the hill where Egbert beat the forces combined against him derived its name from some battle fought long before his time in the days of Vortegern, the British Prince.

There is no record that we are aware of, in existence, by which we have any authority for saying that the Saxon Brothers, Hengist and Horsa were ever in this part of England. Yet it seems not im probable, nor impossible. The records of that time were very imperfect. The principal historian, Witichendus, a Saxon, might not have been acquainted with every minute detail and circumstance of the period of which he wrote. And when we recollect how many monasteries in this country were afterwards burned by the Danes we cannot but conclude that some chronicles or documents that would throw light on our early history, were consumed in the flames. It seems probable that with Hengist and Horsa came the Holes, or men of Hole, and that they permanently settled in Devonshire, giving to many localities their name, such as South Hole, East Hole and Holes-worthy, small towns yet in existence.

It is so remarkable a fact that Hengist-down should lie near Horse-bridge, that it is a strong temptation to fancy those places derived their names from Hengist and Horsa. Let it also be remembered that Vortegern (who leagued with those chiefs, and by his base intrigues and treachery fixed the Saxon yoke on his countrymen) was Earl of Heretage, of Cornwall. The very station he held connected him more particularly with the Cornish Britons and with the people of Devon. That this part of England was the scene of many fierce engagements long before the time of Egbert is proved by historical facts. Many Saxon adventurers crossed the seas and eventually gained a footing in Britain. The Hole family became connected with the family of Egbert who was the Grandfather of Alfred the Great. And, as shown by the table on page 16, are the direct descendants of that monarch. At Tavistock, the early seat of the Holes, is still preserved an ancient tombstone, or memorial stone, supposed to be commemorative of Alfred the Great.

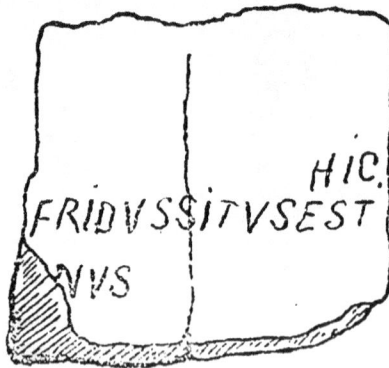

"ALFRIDUS MAGNUS Situs est hic."

There are parts of two words, one immediately below the other, the former ending in *fridus*, the other in *nus*. These probably were ALFRIDUS MAGNUS. The orthography in early times was far from being settled. Anglo-Saxon writers, and among these the King himself, commonly write his name ÆLFRED, and this orthography is frequently followed on ancient coins; in some instances however, as on a coin in the British Museum, the name is written Aelfred; in other writers and on some coins we find Elfred. This respects only the beginning of the word. There was some degree of uncertainty also in the termination. In Smith, "De Republica Anglorum," we find Alfred spelled *Alfredus* and again *Alfridus*. It is probable that this tombstone was removed from his place of sepulture and placed in the Abbey some 20 years after Alfred's death. It is however, not a little remarkable that his remains were transported more than once from the place of their original interment. "His body," says Rapin, "was buried first at Winchester, next removed to the church of the NEW MONASTERY; and lastly his body, monument, church and monastry were all removed without the North Gate of the City, since called The Hide."

In Devonshire the Hole family dwelt until the Norman conquest and the coming of William the Conqueror in 1c66. This monarch gave to Henry Hole an Estate in Exbourne, called HOLE. This estate was near Hatherleigh, in Parish of Exbourne and is still in the possession of the family, the last owner being the Rev. Nathaniel Hole, Rector of Broadwoodsnelly, near that town.

In the Parish of South Tauton, near Ruhampton is also a large estate named HOLE, which for several centuries has been possessed and is still retained by a branch of our family.

In various parts of Devonshire are Manors and Estates bearing this name and which are known, soon after the Norman Conquest, to have belonged to the Hole family.

In the Exeter copy of the Doomsday survey we find that De Holl, or Hole, possessed lands in Cornwall in Wm. 1st's reign. A branch attended Strong-bow (Henry II.) into Ireland, and built a castle in the County of Kilkenney, called after him, CASTLE HOLE.

Another branch was very early settled in the Parishes of Hartland and Exbourne, Devonshire, and we find Richard de Hole possessed of property in former Parish in King John's time.

This gentleman signalized himself in the reign of Richard I, by the capture of some fortified city or town, hence the crest; "a dexter arm, mailed, proper, holding a battle axe and rising from a Mural crown," which was transmitted by him to all his posterity and is borne by them to the present day.

This Richard's son being taken prisoner by Henry III., was obliged to mortgage his estates to Urcal de Exon, (Lyons calls him by this name though others call him Simon) William de Hole being relieved by Richard de Beauple, sold the estates and Exbourne was afterwards repurchased by a descendant and has continued in our family ever since.

The Holes of Clannaborough possessed the Exbourne property in 1629; it then became the property of Peter, son of John Hole; (He also possessed lands called Middlecotts, still in our possession) Peter

Hole dying in 1688 gave to his nephew, Joshua Hole, the property at Exbourne and so it continued, from father to son, to the present generation, the present owner being Mr. N. T. B. Hole.

Several records will here be given that are taken from a careful search of the Registry of the Bishop of London; The Archives of the City of Lincoln and the Archives of the Episcopal Palace at Buckden, in Huntingdonshire, where they are kept with great care and accuracy.

"By an inquisition taken on Thursday next after the Feast of St. Lawrence, Anno 3rd, Henry V, (1416) it was found that Hugh Hole, Knight, was seized of the Manor of Oxey Richard, held of William, Abbot of St. Albans, in right of his church, and *died seized thereof* in the Wednesday next after the Feast of the Apostles Peter and Paul, then last past, leaving his son and heir *Thomas Hole*, of the age of 24 years and upwards."

(Esc.—3—Henry V, N. 41.

"By another inquisition taken on Wednesday next after the Feast of the Conception of the Blessed Virgin Mary, Anno 8th, Henry V, (1421) it was found that THOMAS HOLE, being seized of the Manor of Oxey-Richard, granted the same to Richard Cole, DAVID HOLE, Thomas Heuster and John Wellys, of Watford, to hold them from St. Dunstan's Day, Anno 7th, Henry V. For twenty years, and afterwards Thomas Hole released his right in the Estate to them, whereby they were seized thereof in their demesne as of fee at the time of the death of Thomas Hole who died 21st of November then past, leaving Margery his daughter, aged 2 years and upwards, who married John Troutbeck, 23rd, Henry VI, (1452) and a son EDMUND HOLE, Knight.

(See Esc. II—Henry VI. No. 50.)

The next parochial document appertaining to the Hole family which we will here notice is of great interest and is copied at some length.

"The Account of THOMAS HOLE, warden of the Churche of Tavistocke, ffrom the thirde day of Maye in the yeare of our Lorde Godd one thousande ffyve hundred ffower schore and eight, until the third day of Maye in the yeare of our Lorde Godd one thousand ffyve hundred ffower schore and nyne; that is to weete, for one whole yeare." (1588-1589.)

Receipts for the burhalle and belle. *

"Imprimis, the same accomptant does charge himself with the

---

* This shows that the expression's used by Shakespeare in Hamlet "The bringing home of bell and burial" were in the current form of his day.

receipt of IV pence ffor the greate bell, upon the deathe of Margaret the daughter of Roger Dollyn."

"Item. Receaved upon the deathe of Agnes Drake, for all bells and her grave, VII shillings, IV pence."

"Receaved of the P'shers (Parishoners) of Tavystocke towarde a rate made for the setting fforth of Souldyers for the guardynge of the Queen's Majestie's P'son, and towardes the mayntaunance of the churche this yeare, as appeareth by a book of particulars thereof, XXXII pounds; X shillings; IV pence". A large portion of this charge was doubtless for the musters of 1588, the year of the Spanish Armada.

"Item, gave Mr. Biekell, Mr. Battishill, Mr. Knightes and other preachers who preached at several times in this Parish Church this yeare (1588) IV shill. VIII pence." "Item paide for wyne and bread this yeare for the communion table LIX shillings, III pence." "Item, paide Thomas Watts for amendinge the Bible and the booke of Common Prayer, beinge tornen in dyvers places, II shill. II pence." "Item, paide to three Iryshemen, which hadd a lycense from the Earell (Earl) of Bath, VI pence" to a poore man that collected for the hospital of Saynt Leonards, VI pence."

"Item, payde William Gaye, for killing eight ffoxes this yeare VIII shillings."

"Item, payde for a chayne and setting on thereof for the fastenynge of the *dictionarrie* in the Schole howse, IX pence.

"Item, payde Walter Burges, for one planke and nayles, amendynge of the widow Nicholls and Walter Poynter's wife's seate and other seates, VII pence."

"Payde him for washing of the churches clothes, VIII

"Item, for wrytinge this accompt and the accompt of the Alms-house lands, VI shill., VIII d.

Signed,

"THOMAS HOLE."   { Seal }

This document is of very great interest as being the earliest known writing of any member of the Hole family. The last item contained in Thomas Hole's bill shows a thrifty spirit scarcely equaled by any of the modern bearers of this honored name.

CHAPTER II.

THE HOLES OF CLANNABOROUGH.

The Holes of Clannaborough, already mentioned, were a branch of the Devonshire Hole family and resided in Barnstaple. It is a common saying there that there "are as many Holes in Devon as there are in a rabbit warren."

Of this line was the Right Rev. Richard Hole, 1746-1803, Poet and Antiquary, son of William Hole, Archdeacon of Barnstaple and Canon of Exeter Cathedral, who died in 1791. Richard was educated in the Grammar School at Exeter; was famous for his dry humor and skill in acting; was ordained in the English Church, Curacy of Sowton, near Exeter, which he held till 1777. In 1792, Richard Hole was promoted by the Bishop of Exeter to the rectory of Farringdon, and died at Exmouth, 28th day of May, 1803.

Almost all the Holes of Barnstaple are descended from old Peter Ataller Hole, who died in the year 1547, (38th of Henry VIII,) at the reputed age of 100 years. The said Peter dying in 1547 left a son William Hole, whose dates are not given. William had son Thomas Hole, who died in 1592. Thomas had son John Hole, who survived his father only seven years, and died in 1599. John Hole, (died 1599) had son John Hole of Connaborough, who bought the estate of Middlecot. His father, Nicholas Hole, was called Nicholas of Middlecott. The father of this Nicholas was the Rev. Joshua Hole, 1666, of Hole in Exbourne, whose father was also Joshua, a man of much property and of many estates in Teinistone Hole, Middlecott, Alswear. Hills, Blackmead and Pilcock woods, Died 1705. Joshua had son, Rev. William Hole, Archdeacon of Barnstaple, born 1741, died 1791, before mentioned, whose son Lewis became an Admiral in the British Navy and commanded H. M. S. Kersage at the battle of Trafalgar in 1805. Another son of the Rev. Wm. Hole was Captain Henry Hole, of the Royal Navy. Captain Henry Hole had son, Henry F. Hole, a merchant of New Forge, Ireland, whose son Henry Frederick Hole has been for the past 14 years a resident of Fulton, Florida.

The Clannaborough Holes intermarried with the Berry family and the Berrys are ancestors of the line just traced, they are therefore legitimately entitled to notice in this connection.

THE BERRY FAMILY OF DEVONSHIRE.

From the Worthies of Devon, published in 1701.

Robert Berry, one of the first conquerors of Ireland, was an Englishman, and, as we are informed, a native of Devonshire, and the family of the same name lately at Winscott, near Great Farrington, descended from a younger branch of the Irish stock, whereof this gentleman was the original.   *   *   *

One of which settled his lands in England upon his younger son, whereof a great share lay in this county, for Hallscombe in Winkleigh; Azeton in Ash-reney; Combe in Roxborough; North-Hole and South-Hole in Buckinton-Loges; East-Legh in the Parish of West-Legh and Winscott in the Parish of St. Giles, did anciently belong to the Berrys. For so far back as the first three Edwards, Kings of England; this family possessed a fair inheritance in this Shire, (Devonshire) and "long before their reigns too," Mr. Resdon, (heir of that branch of the family at Winscott) assures us that John Berry of Winscott married the daughter and heir of Jeffrey-Legh, in the days of King John, which is pretty near the time wherein the gentleman of whom we are treating lived.

"This seems to be a confirmation of his being this County-man born: in which, having a plentiful estate, one of his successors sent hither a younger son of his to possess and enjoy it, whose posterity continued here, in worshipful rank, until the last age, (generation)."

"Having now spoken thus largely of the family in general we shall proceed to that eminent person in particular who was the founder thereof, ROBERT BERRY. Cambden tells us that there were two of this name who were very influential in the Conquest of Ireland, viz., Robert Berry and Walter Berry (or Barry). The former of these Robert Berry, by his noble exploits, hath transmitted his name and memory down with great honor to posterity. He was an eminent soldier and wrote his name so deep in the chronicles of both Kingdoms with the point of his sword, that time itself, for these several hundred years, hath not been able to expunge or erase it."

Ireland was the happy stage wherein he acted a noble part; into which he went under the auspicious conduct of the famous Strongbow, Earl of Pembroke, in company of a near relation, his uncle, Fitz-Stephen of Norton, from later lords called Norton-Dawney, near Dartmouth in this County.

This happened in the days of King Henry II. of England, (1154-1189).

The Earl, with those powers he brought with him out of England, made such progress in the Conquest of Ireland that the King (Henry II.), began to grow jealous of him and to suspect his power, so that he put forth his proclamation requiring the said Earl and his adherents, upon grievous penalties to return into England. And here it may not be ungrateful to the reader to interpose the names of those who went out of England with Dermic MacMorrag into Ireland, as I find them recorded by the famous Cambden, (Brit. in Ireland).

> Richard Strong-bow, Earl of Pembroke,
> Robert Fitz-Stephens,
> Maurice Pendergest,
> *Robert Berry,
> Maurice Fitz-Gerald, with Gaulter and
> Alexander, his sons.
> William Notte,
> Hugh DeLacy,
> *Humphrey DeBohun
> Hugh Tirell,
> *Hugh Hole,
> David Walsh,
> *Peter Hole,
> Robert Poer,
> Adam DeGernez,
> Philip DeBreos,
> *Walter DeBerry,
> John DeCurcy,
> Miles of St. Davias,
> And others.

Cambden tells us that Robert Berry was "one who was rather ambitious to be really eminent than to seem so" and that he was the first man wounded in the Conquest of Ireland. His posterity also, for their great loyalty and valour have been honored with the title of Baron Berry and afterwards with that of Viscount Butiphant, by the Kings of England and at this day (1701) with that of Earl of Barrymore, "so by their riches and estate came they to be called by the people, Barry-more or Barry the Great." This family has its chief dwelling or Manor house in the County of Cork, near the great Island, where stands the noble seat called Barry-Court.

"When this honourable person died we are not able at this distance to determine. Some of his posterity flourish in this County at their seat at Winscott at the present day," (1701) and many are in the United States, (1904.) (Crest of the Berry Family, on a torse Argent, and Gules, a Woolf's Head, couped sable)

In England the Holes appear to have been eminent churchmen and to have held high offices in their profession. In the records of

Buckinghamshire we find that Charles Hole Phillips, the eldest son of Carles Phillips and Elizabeth Hole (daughter of Richard Hole) was baptized, March 29th 1678, at Chalfont St. Peters, County Bucks, (Parish Register.) That he was born the same day and was baptized by his great grandfather, the Rev. Thomas Hole, of Caunton, (Generation XXIV), his mother's grandfather, who was buried December 22nd, 1679, aged 90 years. (Parish Register) This was the Rev. Thomas Hole whose *grandson*, Jacob Hole, (XXVI) emigrated to America in 1740.

Another English Prelate of note was the Rev. Matthew Hole, D. D., Rector of Exeter College, Oxford, who was born in Devonshire in the year 1640 and died at Oxford in 1730, aged 90 years. The University of Oxford so highly estimated the Theological writings of Rev. Matthew Hole, that at its own expense, they were reprinted, some 75 years since.

Until the year 1711 there was a Peerage in the Hole family and it would be a problem for President Roosevelt to unravel, in his discussion of Race-Suicide why, when all other branches of the family seemed to flourish and to be uncommonly thrifty, this line should be blighted by the Patent of Nobility and allowed to wither and die. This Peerage was founded by Denzil Hole, who was created, by letters patent dated 20th April, Anno Carolus II—A. D. 1661, Lord Hole of Ifield. He had three wives: first Dorothy, sole heiress and daughter of Sir Francis Ashley of Dorchester, Knight, by whom he had issue four sons, Francis (who succeeded him in the possession of the Manor and Estates); Denzil, John and John, who died in their infancy. His second wife was Jane, eldest daughter and co-heir of Sir John Shirley of Isville, County Sussex, Knight, and widow of Sir Thomas Court, Knight.

His 3rd wife was Hesther, the second daughter, and co-heir of Gideon de Lou, of Columbiers in Normandy, and widow of Jas. Richer, Lord of the Manor of Cambernon, in Normandy, but by neither of these had he any issue. (Dugdale) His son, Francis Hole, of Winterbourne, St. Martin was created a Baronet by patent dated 27th June. 1660, (one year prior to his Father's patent), and upon the death of his father became second Lord Hole of Ifield. He married (1st) Lucy, youngest daughter of Sir Robert Carr of Sleaford, in Lincolnshire, Knight, by whom he had issue Mary and Denzilla, who died infants. His second wife was Anne, eldest daughter and co-heir of Sir Francis Pile of Compton-Beauchamp, by whom he had issue Denzil (who succeeded him). Denzil Hole, 3rd Lord Ifield, died without issue and the Manor and Estates came to John Hole, the great grandson of Sir John Hole of Houghton (Gen. XXIII) (the son of Vicar Hugh Hole, County of Nottingham, Caunton Manor.)

He married Margaret, daughter and co-heir of Henry Cavendish, Duke of Newcastle and was himself created Duke of Newcastle in 1694, which title became extinct at his death on July 15th, 1711. He left an only daughter, Henrietta Cavendish, who married 31st Oct., 1713, the Hon. Edward Harley, 2nd Earl of Oxford. His sister, Grace Hole, married Thomas, Lord Pelham of Laughton, and had issue two sons, Thomas and Henry.

CHAPTER III.

I.—EGBERT, history tells us, was the first King of England; that he
was born about 775, and in 800 ascended the throne of Wessex,
one of the seven kingdoms forming the Heptarchy by which Britain was then governed; that in 827 he had subdued all the other
rulers and became sole monarch of England. He died about 838,
and was succeeded by his son.

II.—ETHELWULF, who ruled until 857, when dying was succeeded by
his four sons in succession. The three elder ones each ruled but
a short time, the youngest of them dying in 871 from the effects
of a wound received in battle with the Danes. Upon his death
the fourth son,

III.—ALFRED, called "Alfred the Great," born in 849 at Wantage,
Berkshire, became king and ruled thirty years, until his death
in October, 901. He married Elswith, daughter of a Mercian
nobleman, by whom he had

IV.—EDWARD, who succeeded his father as king and ruled until his
death in 925. He had three sons, who successively became kings
of England, and a daughter,

V.—EDGINA, who first married Charles III., of France. Charles
died Oct. 7, 926, after which she married Henry, third Count De
Vermandois; by whom she had

VI.—HUBERT, who upon the death of his father became fourth Count
de Vermandois; had

VII.—ADELA, who married Hugh Magnus, the great Count de Vermandois, son of Henry I., *King of France,1031-60, by wife Anne,
daughter of Yaroslav; Grand Duke and ruler of Russia for thirty-
five years, whose wife Adela had

*Henry I. was a son of Robert II. King of France 936-1031 and Con-
stance daughter of the Count of Toulouse; a grandson of Hugh Capet,founder
of the Capetian dynasty, born about 940, crowned July 3, 987, and died October 24, 996; a great grandson of Hugh, the Great Duke of France, who died
in 956, a brother-in-law of Louis IV., fifth king in direct line from Charle-
magne and a great-great grand son of Robert the Strong, who first repulsed
the Northern pirates, prior to 855.

VIII.—ISABEL ,who married Robert de Beaumont first Baron de Bellomont, who became first Earl of Leicester, he died 1118, and she in 1131, had

IX.—ROBERT, second Earl of Leicester, who married Lady Amicia de Ware. He became Lord Justice of England and died 1163; had

X.—ROBERT, third Earl of Leicester, steward of England, who had

XI.—MARGARET, who married Saier de Quincey, created in 1207 Earl of Winchester, and who died in 1219. She had

XII.—ROGER, who became second Earl of Winchester and constable of Scotland. He married Helen, daughter of Alan, Lord of Gallaway, and died in 1264; had

XIII.—ELIZABETH, who married Alexander, Baron Cumyn, Second Earl of Buchan, and had

XIV.—AGNES, who married Gilbert, Baron de Umfraville. She had

XV.—GILBERT, who succeeded his father as Baron de Umfraville, and became governor of the Castle of Forfar. He married Matilda, Countess, of Angus, and died in 1308; had

XVI.—ROBERT, born 1290, second Earl of Angus, who married Lady Eleanor, by whom he had

XVII.—THOMAS, born 1329, Sir Thomas de Umfraville, of Harbottle, who married Joane, daughter of Adam de Rohan and had

XVIII.—THOMAS, Sir Thomas de Umfraville, Lord of Riddesdale, born 1370, who married Lady Agnes, had

XIX.—MARGARET, (1407) married HUGH HOLE (1403).

XX.—WM. HOLE, of South Hole, born 1436, married Joan Cole.

XXI.—NICHOLAS HOLE, born 1477, married Margery Doun (of the Doones of Devonshire).

XXII.—HUGH HOLE, (1520) Vicar of Caunton in 1567, married Cecily Cole, and had issue,

XXIII.—SIR JOHN HOLE, (1566) married a Fortescue of Preston, and had issue,

XXIV.—REV. THOMAS HOLE, born 1589—died 1679 (Parish Register) married Aelanore Douglas and had son,

XXV.—JACOB HOLE, born 1647, who had sons John and Jacob Hole.

XXVI.—JACOB HOLE, born 1689 and Barbara, his wife, came to America in 1740, bringing with them four sons, Peter, John, Charles and Daniel.

XXVII.—CHARLES HOLE, (1728-1803) married Mary McGinnis, (1738-1815); and had issue eleven children.

XXVIII.—Jacob (1758-1842); Nathan (1759-1882); Levi (1761-1803) Rebecca (1763-1825); Mary (1768-1849); David (1770-1854); Jonah (1772-——); John (1774-1784); Ann 1777-1855); Tacy (1779-1828 and Elizabeth (1780-1865).

The posterity and history of the 11 children of Charles and Mary Hole will be given in succeeding chapters.

CHAPTER IV.

THE HOLES OF DEVONSHIRE.

Family seat: South Hole, in Cornwood.

Arms: Gules, a bend lozengy, ermine.

Crest: On a chapeau, falcon, the wings elevated, Argent.

Much of the following material is taken from Heathcote's "Devonshire in 1630" in which valuable work, considerable space is given to the history of the Hole family. The first ancestor, in this line, named by Heathcote is

XIX.—HUGH HOLE, born 1403, who married, in 1434 Margaret, the daughter of Sir Thomas de Umfraville, Lord of Riddesdate, of Harbottle, and Lady Agnes, his wife, born 1407. Of this Ancestor we find no further record except that he had one son,

XX.—WILLIAM HOLE, born 1436, who married Joan, daughter of Simon Cole, Esq., of Slade and had issue, John, Hugh, Nicholas, Baldwin, William and Joan married to John Stert.

First, John married and had issue, Walter, who married Jane, daughter of Thomas Fortescue, of Wimpston in Parish of Modbury, and had issue, John, Hugh, Edward, Thomas, Joan and four other daughters.

Second, Hugh, second son to William of South Hole, married Joan, daughter of Flashmond and had issue, Thomas, Walter, Stephen, John and William.

XXI.—Third, NICHOLAS HOLE, Knight, born 1477, married a daughter of Walter Woodley of Tedburn.St. Mary and had issue, William, John and Joan, married John Cholwich, of Rowden. Nicholas married for his second wife, Margery a daughter of Richard Doun (or Doone) of Holesworthy, and had issue Thomas, Hugh, Walter, John, William, Thomasin who married John Luxton, and Elizabeth who died unmarried.

XXII.—HUGH, born 1520 the fourth son of Sir Nicholas (or the 2nd son by 2nd marriage) took holy orders, entered the Church and became Vicar of Caunton in Nottinghamshire, was known to have been Vicar in the year 1567, will be traced elsewhere.

Sir John Hole, the 4th son, by 2nd marriage of Sir Nicholas, married Mary, daughter of Ellis Warwick and had issue, S.r Warwick Hole, John, Sir Francis, Nicholas, Walter, George, Ellis, Benjamin, Thomas and Philippa, who married Sir Reginald Mohun of Hall, in Cornwall.

Sir Warwick Hole, of Wembury, Knight, Sheriff of Devon, 1618-1619, married Mary, daughter of Halse of Efford. Married for second wife, Margaret, daughter of Sir William Courtenay of Powderham, Knight, and died without issue, Jan. 16, 1625.

Sir Francis, his brother, married Jane, daughter of Rogers of Canington, in Somerset, and had issue, John and one daughter and died in 1622.

John Hole, second son of Nicholas and brother to Hugh, Vicar of Caunton, married Elizabeth, daughter of Thomas Pollexien, of Kitley in Yealmpton, and had issue, Isabel, Agnes, Honor, Charity, Mary, Julyan, Joan, Anne, Margaret and an only son Walter, who married Elizabeth, daughter of William Strode of Newnham and had issue: Arthur, Sampson, Judith, Jane, Joan, (married Thomas Fownes of Plymouth,) Frances, (married John Snelling), Isabel, Agnes, Elizabeth and Susan.

Sampson, the second son, was Sheriff of Devon in the 18th year of Jas. I. (1621), married Joan, daughter of John Glanvile of Tavistock, one of the Justices in the reign of Queen Elizabeth, and had issue, Matthew, John, Sampson, Walter, Francis, William, Arthur, Nicholas, (M. D.), Alice, Elizabeth, Joan and Sarah.

Walter Hole, 5th son of Nicholas, or 3rd by second wife, married Jane, daughter of Thomas Maynard of Brixton, and had issue, Elizeus and Nicholas. Elizeus, Esq., Counsellor-at law and Justice of Peace, married, 1st, a daughter and co-heir of John Hender of Botreaux or Bos-Castle, in Minster, Cornwall, and had issue who all died young; married 2nd, Alice, daughter and co-heir of Bray of Northumberland, the widow of Nicholas Evelegh, fourth son of Geo. Evelegh of Holcombe, in Ottery, St. Mary.

Having disposed of these large families and collateral branches, we will return to our ancestor, HUGH HOLE, Vicar of Caunton.

XXII.—HUGH the 4th son of Sir Nicholas Hole and grandson of Wm. Hole of South Hole in Devonshire, married Cecily, daughter and co-heir of Nicholas Cole of Paignton. Removed from Devonshire to Nottinghamshire, and had issue, John, Margery, Margaret and Elizabeth. While Vicar of Caunton, Hugh Hole became possessed of the Manor of Caunton, a family estate which had for some generations belonged to a branch of the Hole family, his ancestors. The picture here given of the Manor of

Caunton shows the old part of the house and the new wing erected by the present owner, the Very Rev. Samuel Reynolds Hole, Dean of Rochester. This famous home has been owned by the Holes since the year 1249, and is the site of the celebrated "Rose Gardens" of Dean Hole and his lady.

XXIII.—SIR JOHN HOLE, born 1565, only son of Hugh, counsellor-at-law, married a Fortescue of Preston, in Ermington, and had issue, Henry, (died unmarried) Thomas, Josias and Philippa, who married Richard Dean.

XXIV.—REV. THOMAS HOLE, born 1589—died 1679 (Parish Register), married Aelanore Douglas and had issue, Richard and Jacob—

XXV.—JACOB HOLE, born 1647, wife's name not known—had issue, two sons, John who died 1711, and Jacob. John the oldest son remained in England and inherited the Manor of Caunton.* Jacob, the younger son came to America and was the founder of the large family of Holes in the U. S. The family of John Hole will first be traced and the family of the emigrant brother given in another chapter.

PEDIGREE OF HOLES OF CAUNTON MANOR, IN CHURCH OF CAUNTON.

XXVI.—JOHN HOLE, son of Jacob, married Bridget, (last name unknown), and had, with other issue,

XXVII—JOHN HOLE, Baptized April 26, 1713, and had with other issue by Hannah, his wife

XXVIII.—SAMUEL HOLE, Baptized June 28, 1747, who married Sarah, daughter of John Kercheval, Esq., and had with other issue,

XXIX.—SAMUEL HOLE, Baptized Dec. 27, 1778, who married Mary, daughter of Charles Cooke, Esquire, and had, with other issue,

XXX.—SAMUEL REYNOLDS HOLE, born Dec. 5th, 1819, Baptized Dec. 12, 1819, married Caroline, daughter of John Francklin, Esq. and had issue,

XXXI.—SAMUEL HUGH FRANCKLIN HOLE, born Oct. 16, 1862, Baptized Dec. 21, 1862. Married Geraldine, daughter of Charles Markham, Esq., of Tapton House, and his wife Rose, daughter of Sir Joseph Paxton, Knight, has issue,

XXXII.—SAMUEL JOHN MARKHAM HOLE, born 1893, and BRIDGET HOLE.

This closes the record, to date, of the English branch of our family and before tracing the American line we will give some account of the present head of the family in England and of his son Hon. Hugh Francklin Hole.

* Also became 4th Lord Hole of Ifield and Duke of New Castle.

CHAPTER V.

SAMUEL R. HOLE, DEAN OF ROCHESTER.

SAMUEL REYNOLDS HOLE was educated at Brasenose College, Oxford—of which college, by the way, the Deans of York and Manchester are both members—where he graduated in 1844, though he did not proceed to his Master's degree till 1878. He has held no preferment other than that of the curacy, and subsequently vicarage of Caunton, Nottinghamshire, where he lived, one of the most popular of squ'arsons, from 1844 to 1887. Bishop Wordsworth appointed him to the unpaid prebendal stall of North Kelsey, in Lincoln Cathedral, in 1875, and two years previously made him Rural Dean of Southwell. He sat for four years in Convocation as Proctor for the Clergy, first of Lincoln and then of Southwell, till in 1887 the Marquis of Salisbury nominated him for the Deanery of Rochester, vacant by the death of Dean Scott.

About half of Mr. Hole's ministry of forty-three years in the quiet village of Caunton in the Midlands was passed like that of any other well-to-do kindly country squ'arson of a byegone age. He fulfilled, with scrupulous fidelity, the routine and accustomed duties of his office, and the temporal wants of the poor were always his care. But there was, as he has himself related, no special zeal for souls—nay, not even a knowledge of the great natural power within him for the good of others. He was always fond of a joke, and is the author, to the present day, of many a first-rate pun. He enjoyed the friendship of Leech, who illustrated his first book, "A Little Tour in Ireland," published in 1858, and is said to have been the only clergyman present at the weekly dinners where the contents of the next number of *Punch* were arranged. The Dean was always fond of travel, and in 1840 published a chatty book, "Nice and Her Neighbours." He was, and is, as every one knows, passionately fond of roses, the cultivation of which queen of flowers was one of his great delights at Caunton, while he frequently went about the country judging roses at great shows. His "Book about Roses," published in 1869, is still a standard work on the subject, being alike educational and chatty.

When the Church movement became a power in the country—especially when the Bishops of Lichfield and Truro, Canons Body and Knox Little, devoted themselves to mission work—the heart of the vicar of Caunton was stirred within him, and he began to take great interest in the crusade against evil which he saw on every side around him. The appointment of Bishop Wordsworth to the see of Lincoln quickened his growing zeal; and the keen discrimination of that illustrious prelate soon saw the value of one whose commanding presence and natural ability, joined now with a burning love for souls, was somewhat lost in a country village. Mr. Hole is said to have first discovered his preaching powers when the light failed him in a strange country church, and he was compelled to abandon his manuscript one dark Sunday afternoon. Gradually his fame as a preacher spread, and he began to take part in mission work in which he became a great adept, and in 1880 he published his most useful work, "Hints to Preachers, with Sermons and Addresses." Up and down the land, in nearly every cathedral and large church, the manly voice, the common-sense utterances, and eloquent pleading for all that is good and true, of Dr. Hole, have become household words, and his influence is especially great over men. He has taken a very warm interest in the Church of England Working Men's Society, on whose behalf one of his ablest sermons in St. Paul's Cathedral was delivered.

At the midday services at St. Paul's Cathedral he attracts men of all grades of the middle class; but perhaps his most noteworthy achievement is his filling—alone of any preacher—St. Nicholas, Liverpool, daily during the week he preaches in Lent to business men. That he has made his influence felt at Rochester none can doubt, but the Archbishop of Canterbury who, by making him his chaplain gave the sanction of his authority to mission work, might do worse than whisper to Mr. Balfour that, owing to his physical energy and good health, the Dean is not too old to be appointed to a yet higher dignity.

Both Dean Hole and his son were educated at Brasenose College, Oxford. (The Dean says that the name is derived from *Brasen Ans.* King Alfred's Brewhouse) and if that learned Monarch knew no more about brewing than he did about baking, there must have been some wry faces over the royal cakes and ale).

Samuel Reynolds Hole married in 1861, Caroline, eldest daughter of John Fraucklin, Esq. of Nottinghamshire (Gonalson), their only child, Samuel Hugh Francklin Hole is a Barrister at Law and resides in Portman Square, London.

In May 1903 the writer, accompanied by James Franklin Keeler, visited Dean Hole at the Deanery in Rochester, England. They were most kindly welcomed and hospitably entertained. The Dean is an enthusiastic autograph collector and finding a sympathetic Scrutator, he exhibited his Autographic treasures, consisting of the valued correspondence with John Leech, Charles Dickens, Thackery, Gladstone and almost all the prominent English men and women of letters of the past 50 years. The Deanery gardens and the Cathedral were visited and the objects of historic interest were pointed out and explained by the Dean. While at the dinner table Mrs. Hole remarked that the part of the house where we were eating had been occupied for over six hundred years. It was a remarkable and beautiful mansion and had been visited by Queen Elizabeth and several other monarchs. After dinner Dean Hole and General Forbes, of the British Army, each of them in their 84th year, played several games at Bowles, on the fine Deanery bowling grounds, while Mrs. Hole entertained her guests by showing them the silver, the paintings and the art-treasures of the Deanery and Cathedral.

While in Rochester we were permitted to sleep in the bed once occupied by Queen Victoria, and were taken to visit the haunts of Dickens and the house in which he died, at Gad's Hill, some three miles from the City.

Dean Hole is known in England and America as an author, a wit and humorist, and as The King of the Roses. He is six feet four inches in height and of a most commanding presence. When in the United States, a few years ago, a Cincinnati paper said of him, "Dean Hole is certainly the finest specimen of Elizabethan ecclesiastical architecture that England has ever sent to this country, the reverend gentleman, seventy-five years old and over six feet tall, walked up two flights of stairs to his room at the hotel *with the hardy appearance and exact posture of a young Indian* in preference to using the elevator, notwithstanding that he had just endured the exhaustion of a ride from Chicago. He is as remarkable a man to look at as he is in the church affairs in England, and his long gray hair is combed back from a strong Scotch cast of features." The Dean says 'his only center of gravity is the pulpit,' and he is best described as large and ruddy, with white hair and very keen, kindly, quizzical eyes that are perpetually smiling, even when the rest of his face is serious.

As a humorist Dean Hole is sometimes called the "Mark Twain of England," and he has a sincere regard for his old friend "Bill Nye." Bill Nye was living when the Dean was in the States in 1894 and after his return to England "Bill" wrote the following letter which, says the Dean, "expresses so exactly and incisively the justification of humor, to which I have tried to conform, that I asked and received permission to publish it."

Christmas Day, Washington, 1894.

My Dear Dean Hole:—You do not realize, perhaps, that you had a mission to America, which I am going to appropriate mostly to myself.

I have always sort of wondered why "the children of a king" should 'go mourning all their days,' and I have often tried to settle in my own mind the question why the clergymen and the man who rides a bicycle should never smile.

It seems to me that if I could be as good as many preachers appear to be, I would be radiant with gladness all the time. You have proved to me that a clergyman may have a good time, good health and long life, without injury to his piety. It is fully as unjust to put down all clergymen as enemies to humor as it would be to assume that all humorists were destitute of religion. So you see, my dear friend, that the general public has a wrong idea of both of us. I have rebelled more perhaps over this assumption than 'most any other. Why should one who sees and describes the ridiculous side of life be necessarily vulgar and Godless? On the the other hand, why should one whose mission it is to proclaim the gladdest of all glad tidings, as did the angels 1894 years ago, be habitually dejected and bilious?

To me your life, as revealed in your "Memories," seems almost ideal, and I am proud and happy if, along with those delightful friends of whom you write, on the shelf devoted to your American acquaintances, you may find room for your sincere friend,

"EDGAR W. NYE.,

Dean Hole is the author of some dozen volumes on Rose Culture, Gardening, Travels, Memoirs and Memories, Lectures to Working Men, etc., etc.

His "Book about Roses" has been through some 15 editions and has been popular in England for almost forty years. "A Book About the Garden and the Gardener" is a profusion of jokes and good stories, with a vein of serious thought running through the whole.

His "Addresses to Working Men" are excellent, direct, simple and manly. The book is useful both for the sensible counsel it gives and for serving as a model of directness for young speakers.

The St. James Gazette says of his "More Memories," "There is a touch of Oliver Wendell Holmes about the volume, which is particularly striking in the chapter in which Dean Hole reprints some of his poetry, humorous and otherwise." *The Spectator* said, "Dean Hole was the intimate friend of Leech; he enjoyed the companionship of Thackery; he has been an honorary member of the fellowship which surrounds the Table of Mr. Punch. It might warm the most frigid disestablish-mentarian toward the Church of England to find a Dean with such a keen sense of humor, with such kindly tolerance. He tells a good story with a relish which is a veritable inspiration. His tastes are wide, embracing literature and art, horticulture and most branches of sport."

The Oxonian who accompanied John Leech in his famous "Little Tour in Ireland," and who wrote the account which was illustrated by Leech in his happiest and most successful manner, was the present Dean of Rochester. This book, one of the Dean's best, was out of print for nearly thirty years until quite recently republished in London, when it had an enormous sale.

The two poems here published are of great interest, as the one was the hymn sung over the dead body of the Queen, as it lay in state, while the other is probably the good Dean's expression of his trust for his only son, at that time a soldier in South Africa.

God rest our Queen.

———

Borne by Thy angels, through the awful way,
To Paradise, where dawns the eternal day,—
    God rest our Queen.

Faith dares not doubt; her prayer and ours is heard;
She claims the precious promise of thy word,—
    God rest our Queen.

With those her dearest, whom she mourned so long,
She lives, and loves, and learns the triumph song,—
    God rest our Queen.

Glory to Jesus—there remaineth still
This rest for all, who seek to do his will—
    God rest our Queen.

                    S. REYNOLDS HOLE.

January 23, 1901.

HYMN FOR TIME OF WAR.

If their enemy besiege them in the land of their cities, what prayer
and supplication be made by any man, which shall know the plague of
his own heart, then hear Thou in Heaven, Thy dwelling place, and
forgive.—I KINGS, VIII, 38.

Father, forgive Thy children come to claim
The pardon promised to their grief and shame;
Forgetful, thankless, in their wayward will;
Father, Thou knowest, and Thou lovest still.

Love warns and chastens, love rebukes their pride,
Who in themselves and not in Thee confide;
Though vast our armies, and our quarrel just,
Thine all the Power, in Thee be all our trust.

Be with us, GOD of battles, in this fight;
Ourselves are sinful, but our cause is right;
Be with our soldiers, arm them, heart and mind,
In danger dauntless, but in conquest kind.

Pity the wounded, be they friend or foe,
And help their helpers in the hours of woe;
Bless all, O Christ, who do Thy gracious will,
Bless the kind nurse, and bless the surgeon's skill.

GOD of the widow, soothe her sore distress,
Be Thou the Father of the fatherless,
And teach the mother, mourning for her son,
To pray Christ's prayer, Thy will, not mine, be done.

Inspire Thy priests with wisdom from above,
To tell the dying of Thy deathless love,
To tell brave hearts that Duty, beaten down
And vanquished here, shall win the victor's crown.

DEAN HOLE.

SAMUEL HUGH FRANCKLIN HOLE, Barrister at Law of the Inner Temple, of Caunton Manor Nottinghamshire and of Portman Square, London, is the only son of the very Rev. Samuel Reynolds Hole, Dean of Rochester and of Caroline Francklin, his wife. He was named for the first Hugh Hole, of Caunton, who was Vicar of Caunton in the year 1567, being the first Vicar appointed after the Reformation; for his grandfather, Samuel Hole, of Caunton, who died in 1868, at the age of 90; and for his grandfather Franklin, a near relative of Sir John Franklin, of Arctic fame. This wholesale consumption of family names, which would look like "flying in the face of Providence," began and ended with the naming of little Samuel Hugh Franklin on Oct. 16th, 1862. He was the last but never the least of his race. When visited by the writer in May, 1903, the mighty Barrister and soldier was 6 feet 5½ inches in heighth and crowned this altitude with a lofty silk hat.

He enlisted at the age of twelve years in the Eaton College volunteers with whom he served five years, getting the first five years star, awarded to any member of the corps, was transferred to a Lieutenantcy in the county Battalion of the Nottinghamshire Volunteers with whom he served ten years and was then transferred to a Captaincy in the Royal Sherwood Forresters (Notts. Militia). He resigned on being called to the Bar, but volunteered for South Africa "in Colenso Week." He recruited eighteen personal friends as cyclists (averaging six feet high and forty inches around the chest, nine of whom had rowed head of the river at either Oxford or Cambridge) was sworn in as a private soldier on Jan. 1st, 1900; promoted Lieutenant Jan. 3d, took part in all engagements with his regiment up to the fall of Pretoria, including Hout wek, Lindley, Vet River, Heillran and the engagement at Johannesburg. He was thereafter placed on the staff of the Military Governor of the Orange River Colony as Secretary, Crown Prosecutor and Press Censor. He served also as Provost Marshal and Deputy Adjutant General (See "1000 miles with C. I. V."). He was placed in charge of Mrs. President Steyn, at her own request and was subsequently captured by Boer Patrol while out on an errand of mercy, attempting to bring in a Boer woman and her family to the Refugee Camp. He was tried by Boer Court Marshal and acquitted. He served until the Military governor was superseded by a Civilian Governor, and returned to England in 1901. Mr. Hole has a perfect arsenal of weapons captured in South Africa and delighted his American friends with an exhibition of his military treasures which include the writing desk of President Steyn of the Orange River Colony; the President's easy chair, and a collection of coins fresh from the Pretoria mint, captured when Pretoria was taken and apparently kept for the benefit of his visitors as they were freely offered to us as mementos of our visit.

Mrs. Hole was the daughter of Charles Markham, Esq., of Tapton House and of Rose, his wife, who was the daughter of Sir Joseph Paxton, Knight. There are two interesting children in Mr. Hole's beautiful home in Portman Square: The little Bridget, and Samuel John Markham Hole, (another instance of the English prodigal use of family names). These children are the only descendants of the Dean of Rochester and have probably inherited, with additions and variations, the literary, military, clerical and forensic abilities of their father and grandfather, the Very Rev. Samuel Reynolds Hole and the brilliant and handsome Barrister, Samuel Hugh Francklin Hole.

CHAPTER VI.

1ST GENERATION.—William I, (the Conqueror) King of England crowned 1066, died 1087, married Matilda, daughter of Baldwin, Count of Flanders, had issue,

2ND.—Henry I, King of England, died 1135, married Matilda, daughter of Malcolm III, King of Scotland and had issue,

3RD.—Matilda, (or Maud) married in 1127 Geoffrey Plantagenet, Count of Anjoie and had issue,

4TH.—Henry II, King of England, (died 1189), married Eleanor, daughter of William, Duke of Aquitaine, and had issue,

5TH.—John, King of England, (died 1216), married Isabel, daughter of Aymer, Count of Angouleme, had issue,

6TH.—Henry III, King of England, (died 1272) married Eleanor, daughter of Raymond, Count of Provence, and had issue,

7TH.—Edward I, King of England, (died 1307), married Eleanor, daughter of Ferdinand III, King of Castile, and had issue,

8TH.—Edward II, King of England, died 1327, married Isabel, daughter of Philip IV, King of France and had issue,

9TH.—Edward III, King of England, died 1377, married Philippa, daughter of William, Count of Hainault, had issue,

10TH.—Thomas, Duke of Gloucester, known as Thomas of Woodstock, who married Eleanor de Bohun, daughter of Humphrey, Earl of Hereford, Essex and Northampton, High Constable of England, had issue,

11TH.—Anne of Woodstock, who married William, Earl of Essex, and had issue,

12TH.—(1) William, Lord Fitzwarin, (2) Henry, Earl of Essex and (3) Hon. Lord Berners. William, Lord Fitzwarin had son,

13TH.—Sir Fulke Burgchier, Lord Fitzwarin, who had issue,

14TH.—Elizabeth Burgchier Fitzwarin, who married Sir Edward Stanhope and had issue,

15TH.—(1) Anne, Duchess of Somerset and (2) Margaret, who married Sir William Askew, Lincolnshire, had issue,

16TH.—Anne Askew, (born 1521), married a Kyme, divorced and burned as a heretic, July 26, 1546, had issue,

17TH.—William Askew, had son, (inherited Marsh Grange from Sir Hugh Askew.)

18TH.—John Askew, John had two sons and one daughter,

19TH.—Margaret Askew, born 1613, married Thomas Fell and 2nd George Fox.

20TH.—Sarah Fell, 1643-1714, married William Meade, 1627-1713.

21ST.—Sir Nathaniel Meade, 1684-1760,

22ND.—Wm. Meade married Ellen Worrell,

23RD.—Hannah Meade, married Captain John Thomas,

24TH.—Mary Thomas, 1757-1849, married Jacob Hole.

This line from William the Conqueror has been well known as far back as the 15th generation, but little was known of Margaret Stanhope the mother of Anne Askew, until the writer found the tomb of her sister, Anne Duchess of Somerset, in Westminster Abbey, and from the lengthy epitaph and pedigree there engraved was enabled to fully and completely trace the line to Thomas, Duke of Gloucester, known as Thomas of Woodstock. He, being in the royal line, was easily traced back to William and thus the line is completed. Anne, Duchess of Somerset, the Aunt of Anne Askew was, says Sir John Hayward, "A mannish or rather a devilish woman, for any imperfectibilities intolerable, but for pride monstrous, exceeding subtile and violent. If Margaret Stanhope, Anne's Sister, was of this same disposition we can the more easily account for the treatment of Anne Askew, her daughter, who bore her aunt's name and was forsaken by her parents and husband on account of her religious views. As the inscription and the tomb of the Old Duchess of Somerset are of great importance in establishing the family genealogy it will be here noticed at lenght.

An Alabaster effigy of the Duchess in her robes lies under a recessed arch with richly decorated soffit.

"Anne, Duchess of Somerset, widow of the Protector Somerset, sister-in-law to Queen Jane Seymour and aunt by marriage to Edward VI. Her eldest son, Lord Hertford, in this doleful duty, careful and diligent, doth consecrate this monument to his dead parent."

"Anne rendered this life at 90 years of age on Easter-day, 6th of April, 1587."

"Anne Seymour, a princess descended of noble lineage, being daughter of the worthie Knight SIR EDWARD STANHOPE, by Elizabeth his wyfe, that was daughter of Sir Foulke Burghchier, Lord

Fitzwarin, from whom our moderne Earles of Bath are spronge. Sonne was he unto William, Lord Fitzwarin, that was brother to Henry, Earle of Essex and Hon. Lord Berners, whom William their sire, sometime Earle of Ex. in Normandy, begat of Anne, the sole heire of Thomas of Woodstock, Duke of Gloucester, younger sonne to the mighty Prince King Edward III and of his wyfe Alenore, co-heire unto the 10th Humphrey de Bohun that was Earle of Hereford, Essex and Northampton, High Constable of England."

"Many children bare this Lady unto her Lord, of either sort to witte, Edward, Earle of Hertford, Henry and a younger Edward, Anne, Countess of Warwicke, Margaret, Jane, Mary Katharine and Elizabeth."

Near this tomb is another of great interest to the members of the Hole family. This is the monument to Eleanor de Bohun—our direct ancestress. In the centre of the Chapel is a low altar tomb with the finest brass in the Abbey, "To Eleanore (or Alianore) Duchess of Gloucester—died 1399—the greatest heiress in England, whose husband, uncle to Richard II, was arrested and treacherously murdered at his nephew's instigation. After this "melancholy accident she spent the remainder of her widowhood in the nunnery at Borking." She is represented in her widow's dress, under a triple canopy. Most of the inscription, in brass letters, with heraldic devices, remains around the ledge.

The Seymour family, (Earls of Somerset) were in so many ways connected with the ancestors of the Holes that the various intermarriages must here be noticed.

1st.—SIR EDWARD SEYMOUR, was elevated to the peerage as Viscount Beauchamp, June 5th, 1536, and was created Earl of Hertford, October 18th, 1537.

Two years later he was appointed Lord-great-Chamberlain of England for life. Created Baron Seymour, Feb. 15, 1546, and the next day advanced to the Dukedom of Somerset. He became Protector of the Realm and governor of King Edward VI during his minority. He married Anne (daughter of Sir Edward Stanhope) whose epitaph has been given at some length on a preceding page. She was sister to Margaret—the mother of our Ancestress Anne Askew and her daughter Jane Seymour married Sir Hugh Askew, of Kelsey, in Lincolnshire, the brother of Anne Askew, and her own first cousin. Sir Hugh Askew and Lady Jane Seymour died childless and their possessions were inherited by Anne Askew's son, William Askew. The house called Marsh Grange, of which a picture is given in this volume, thus came into the possession of Anne's son and it was here that his Granddaughter, Margaret Fell, was born in 1613.

2nd.—JANE SEYMOUR, sister of Sir Edward Seymour, married

King Henry VIII and was the mother of King Edward VI. Thus Sir Hugh Askew's wife and Anne Askew's mother were closely allied to the Royal family and this is the explanation of the old tradition that the Holes were related to King Edward VI. Anne Askew, our Ancestress, was indeed *closely related* to the Somerset family (Seymours) but was not a *descendant*.

3rd.—ANNE ASKEW, niece of the Protector Somerset and of Anne, his wife, was the daughter of Sir William Askew, of South Kelsey, in Lincolnshire. She was born in 1521 and burned at the stake, by order of King Henry VIII, on July 26, 1546. We cannot do better than to here give the opinion of two or three eminent writers of that period on the martyrdom of Anne Askew. Bishop Burnet says, "Of Anne Askew it is recorded that she was remarkable both for beauty and for wit and had been educated beyond what was ordinary in that age for her sex. Her husband was one of the Kymes of Lincolnshire and finding that his wife favored the doctrine of the Reformation, he drove her from his home, though she had borne him two children and her conduct was unexceptionable. Abandoned by her husband she came up to London, in order to procure a divorce and to make herself known to that part of the Court who either professed, or were favourably inclined towards Protestantism. But as Henry VIII, with the consent of Parliament, had just enacted the law of the "Six Articles," commonly called "The Bloody Statute," she was cruelly betrayed by her husband and upon his information, taken into custody and examined concerning her faith.

The Act above mentioned denounced death against all heretics or those who should deny the doctrine of transubstantiation, or say that the bread and wine made use of in the sacrament were not changed by consecration into the body and blood of Christ; or maintain the necessity of receiving the sacrament in both kinds; or affirm that it was lawful for Priests to marry; that the law of celibacy might be broken; that private masses were of no avail and that auricular confession to a Priest was not necessary to Salvation. Upon these articles Anne Askew was examined by the Inquisitors, and to all their queries gave proper and pertinent answers, but not being such as they approved she was sent back to prison where she remained eleven days and was denied the small consolation of a friendly visit. The King's Council being at Greenwich she was examined by Chancellor Wriothsley, Gardener, Bishop of Winchester, Drs. Cox and Robinson, who not being able to convince her, sent her to the Tower.

Strype, from an authentic paper, gives the following short account of her examination. "Sir Martin Bowers, (Lord Mayor) sitting with the council, as most meet for his wisdom, and seeing her stand upon life and death." "I pray you," quoth he, "My

Lords give me leave to talk to this woman." (Leave was granted.) "Thou foolish woman, sayest thou that the Priest cannot make the holy body of Christ?

Anne Askew. "I say so my Lord, for I have read that God made man, but that man made God I never read; nor, I suppose, ever shall read it."

Lord Mayor. "No, thou foolish woman, after the words of consecration is it not the Lord's body?"

Anne Askew. "No, it is but consecrated bread, or sacramental bread."

Lord Mayor. "What if a mouse eat it after consecration, what shall become of this mouse?

What sayest thou, thou foolish woman?"

Anne Askew. "What shall become of her *say you*, my lord?"

Lord Mayor. "I say that the mouse is damned."

Anne Askew. "Alack, poor mouse!"

At which answer many ot the council could not refrain from laughing, nevertheless proceeding to put her to the cruel torture of the rack.

Thomas Fuller, the famous church historian, says of the Askew family, "William Ascough was descended of a worshipful and very ancient family now living at Kelsey, Lincolnshire. (The variation of a letter importing nothing to the contrary. I have seen at Sarisbury, his arms, with Allusion to the Arms of that house and some episcopal addition. Such likeness is with me a *better evidence* than *the sameness*, knowing that the clergy in that age delighted to disguise their *Coats* from their *paternal bearings*.)

He was bred Doctor of Laws, a very able man in his profession. Became Bishop of Sarum, Confessor to King Henry VI, and was the first of Bishops who discharged that office, as then conceived beneath the place. Some will say, if King Henry answered the character commonly received of his sanctity, his confessor had a very easy performance. Not so! for always the most conscientious are the most scrupulous in the confession of their sins and the particular enumeration thereof. Bishop Askew was foully murdered before the High Altar at Salisbury, on June 29, 1450, almost 100 years before his grand niece, Anne Askew, was burned at the stake in Smithfield." Of Anne Askew or Ascough, Fuller says, under the heading of MARTYRS, "Anne Askew, daughter of Sir William Askew, Knight, was born in Lincolnshire; of her piety and patience when first *wracked* in the Tower, then burned at Smithfield, I have largely treated in my church History," "She went to Heaven in a Chariot of Fire—July, 26, 1546."

Bishop Bale has preserved a hymn which Anne Askew composed

and sang when she was imprisoned at Newgate. From it the following stanzas are extracted:

"Like as the armed knyght,
Appoynted to the field,
With this world will I fyght,
And faythe shall be my shielde.

Faythe is that weapon stronge
Which will not fail at neede;
My foes therefore amonge
Therewith will I procede.

Faythe in the fathers olde
Obtayned righteoysenuss,
Which makes me verye bolde,
To feare no worlde's distresse.

I now rejoice in hart,
And hope byds me do so;
For Christ wylt take my part,
And ease me of my wo.

Thou sayst, Lorde, whoso knocke,
To them wilt thou attende;
Undo therefore the locke,
And thy strong power sende.

On Thee my care I cast,
For all their cruel spyght;
I set not by their haste,
For thou art my delyght.

I am not shee that lyst
My anker to let fall
For everye dryslyng myst,
My shippe's substanciall."

Her feelings are expressively portrayed in the following stanzas composed while she was in Newgate.

Not oft used I to wryght
In prose nor yet in ryme,
Yet will I shewe one syght
That I saw in my tyme.

I saw a royal throne,
Where justice should have sytt,
But in her stede was one
of Moodye crueil wytt.

Absorbt was rightwysnesse,
As of the ragynge floude,
Sathan, in hys excess,
Sucte up the gylteless flood.

Then, thought I Jesus Lorde,
When thou shalt judge us alle,
Harde is it to recorde
On these men what will fall.

> Yet, Lorde, I Thee desire,
> For that they do to me,
> Let them not taste the hyre
> Of their inyquity."

When Wriothsley and Gardiner failed to frighten their victim into recantation by the threat of the stake or by cross questioning her to lead her to implicate others, they determined on trying the rack.

The account given by Fox, of the prisoner's cruel treatment in the Tower adds a few particulars not yet stated. "First she was let down into a dungeon where Sir Anthony Knevet, the lieutenant, commanded his jailor to pinch her with the rack. Which being done as much as he thought sufficient he went about to take her down, but *Wriothsley the Chancellor*, not contented that she was loosed so soon, confessing nothing, *threw off his gown* and played the tormentor himself. Quietly and patiently praying she abode their tyranny till her bones and joints were almost plucked asunder, so that she was carried away in a chair." "I saw her" said Mr. Loud, tutor to Sir Richard Southwell, "and must needs confess of Mrs. Askew, that the day afore her execution, and the same day also, she had on an angel's face and a smiling countenance, though when the hour of darkness came, she was so racked that she could not stand but was holden up between two serjents."

The time chosen for the close of the tragedy was evening, so that the scene, as night approached, should become more terriffic.

She was brought into Smithfield in a chair because she could not go on her feet. She was tied by a chain to the stake. When all things were thus prepared Dr. Shaxton, who was appointed to preach, began his sermon. Anne Askew hearing and answering unto him, where he said well confirming the same; where he said amiss "There," said she, "he speaketh contrary to the Book."

"The sermon being ended, the martyrs standing there, tied at three several stakes, ready to their martyrdom, began their prayers. The multitude of people was great, the place where they stood being railed to keep out the press. Upon the bench by St. Bartholomew's Church sat Wriothsley, Chancellor of England; the old Duke of Bedford; the old Duke of Norfolk; the Lord Mayor and others." "Then Wriothsley sent to Anne Askew letters offering her the King's pardon if she would recant, refusing to look upon them she made this answer, "I came not hither to deny my Lord and Master."

Whereupon the Lord Mayor commanded fire to be put unto them; and cried in a loud voice. "Fiat Justitia." And thus died the good Anne Askew, with these blessed martyrs, being compassed in with flames of fire, she slept in the Lord leaving behind a singular example of Christian constancy for all men to follow.

—37—

Anne Askew's martyrdom occurred on the 26th of July, 1546, in the 25th year of her age. Her tutor, John Lacels, was one of the three men who suffered at the same time.

Foxe says, "It happened well for them that they died together with Mrs. Askew; for though they were strong and stout men, yet through the exhortation and example of her, being emboldened, they received the greater comfort in that painful kind of death."

Anne Askew resumed her maiden name after being driven from her home by her husband, and no historian has so much as recorded his name, except to say that he was a son of "Old Master Kyme" and had been engaged to marry Anne's older sister. In order to secure a large fortune, her father forced her into this unhappy marriage. Her son William Askew became the heir of his uncle, Sir Hugh Askew, as before stated, and lived at Seaton Priory and Marsh Grange. At the latter home his son, John Askew, was born, and in 1613, at Marsh Grange, was born John's daughter Margaret, afterwards the wife of George Fox, and "the Mother of the Society of Friends."

CHAPTER VII.

The residence of the Fell family was situated in that detached part of Lancashire called "Furness" which lies north of Morecombe Bay. The waters, of which the windows of their house commanded a prospect, penetrate into the land to a depth of some fifteen miles.

This outlying section of Lancashire was long under the government of the monks of Furness Abbey. The Abbey itself was founded A. D. 1127 by King Stephen. The Abbot was sort of King inside these territories, as well as landlord and agriculturalist. At length came the dissolution of the monasteries in 1537, and with that came also grants of monastic land to royal favorites. Swarthmoor Hall became a center of interest about the middle of the seventeenth century. This celebrated mansion stands about a mile south of Ulverstone, in view of mountains, woods and waters, that give great beauty to the scenery. The name of Swarthmoor has been attributed by Bishop Gibson and afterwards by almost all the writers on history of Furness, to Swartz, the Flemish General, who was sent by Margaret of Burgundy to assert the cause of the House of York against the title of Henry VII. He was said to have given his name to the moor on which he mustered his forces. This however can be shown to be erronious, for in Doomsday Book the place is styled "Martz" and in another ancient document "Mart," both being probably the Anglo-Norman style of spelling the Saxon "Worth"or "Wark" meaning a house or enclosed stronghold. It seems to be clear that this estate was formed by purchase of lands held by distinct titles and that a house suitable to the newly constructed property, was built shortly after the Reformation, by the Fells or their predecessors. The estate thus formed was certainly one of the most considerable, and the family, whatever their origin, one of the most wealthy in Furness. So late as the times of Henry VIII the Saxon families of High Furness lived in villages and hamlets of their own name. Of these were probably the Fells, deriving their name from the district of Furness Fells, the general name for High Furness, of whom there were many families both in the position of tenants of the manor and of free homages. Of the latter, one family, the Fells of Redmen Hall, had been known to have been there for nineteen generations, (Baines, Vol. 4.)

At some period or other which we cannot now ascertain, our ancestor, Thomas Fell, became an extensive purchaser of the Abbey lands, covering many hundred acres to the south and west of the paternal estate (Hawkswell) to Morecomb Bay, and at an advanced age he became possessed of a large estate in Kirkly Irelith, the property of the Askews of Marsh Grange, so that his estate extended quite across the peninsula and must, with the outlying farms have been, with the exception perhaps of that of the Prestous of the Abbey, by far the most considerable in Furness. Mr. Fell was educated for the profession of the law and the first mention we find of him is in the year 1641 at the breaking out of the civil war between the King and Parliament. In that year we find him recorded as a "Parliamentarian" along with Sir Thomas Stanley, Standish, Egerton and others of note.

"In the year 1643, a battle was fought in the immediate neighborhood of Mr. Fell's residence, in which he was probably present."

I find this extremely doubtful sentence in an ancient history, but I do not take it to be a reflection upon the bravery and valor of our ancestor Thomas Fell. It was probably meant to intimate that Judge Fell was a soldier and in the battle. If he was not, it is recorded of him elsewhere that he was an exceeding courageous man and rather than renounce his faith or convictions would suffer any sort of persecution.

He became a successful barrister, was afterwards raised to the bench, and was one of the Judges who went the circuit of West Chester and North Wales. He was Vice Chancellor of the County Palatine of Lancaster, Chancellor of the Duchy Court of Westminster, and a county magistrate. He was sent to Parliament as a representative of Lancaster in 1645, along with Sir Thomas Bendloss. During the latter years of Cromwell's administration he retired from Parliamentary life. As a mark of special regard Cromwell presented Judge Fell with a silver cup which was long preserved in the family.* Still Judge Fell looked with disfavor on some of the proceedings of the Cromwellian government, and kept aloof from close association with its chief.

In the year 1632 Thomas Fell married Margaret Askew, the great grand daughter of Anne Askew, the Martyr. Margaret Askew had been both religiously and intellectually well educated for that time. She was in her eighteenth year when she became the mistress of Swarthmoor Hall, her husband in his thirty-fourth.

* The writer also possesses a silver candlestick that belonged to Thomas and Margaret Fell, and has been handed down through successive generations. There are other articles of silverware bearing the Fell name, yet in the possession of various members of the Hole family.

To Thomss and Margaret Fell were born eight children, seven daughters and one son, whose descendants will be given later.

Judge Fell died Oct. 8th, 1658, about one month after Cromwell's death, and a copy of his will is here presented.

The will of Thomas Fell, of Swarthmoor Hall, in the Parish of Ulverston, in the County of Lancaster, Esquire, proved 4th Dec., 1658. (Extracted from the Registry of the Prerogative Court of Canterbury.)

"The twenty-third day of September in the year of our Lord God One thousand, six hundred and fifty eight. Be it remembered that the day and year before written Thomas Fell, of Swarthmoor in the County of Lancaster, Esquire, being sick and weak in body, but of a perfect memory and understanding, blessed be the Lord for the same, doth hereby declare and publish his last Will and Testament in manner and form following; that is to say, I do hereby appoint, nominate and ordain Richard Radcliffe, yeoman, and Timothy Coulton, yeoman, both my menial servants, to be my executors, jointly and severally; nevertheless upon this trust and confidence and to the end and purpose following; that is to say, that after my debts, legacies and funeral expenses be discharged, then they shall dispose and give the rest, residue and overplus of all my real and personal estate, unto my seven daughters, Margaret, Bridget, Isabella, Sarah, Mary, Susanna and Rachel, equally to be divided amongst them. First, I give and bequeath unto the most aged and impotent and necessitous persons within the parish of Ulverstone, the sum of ten pounds, to be distributed by my executors, taking the information and assistance of the overseers of the poor within the said parish. Secondly, I give and bequeath unto the overseers of the said parish for the time being, thirty pounds, with the interest whereof they are to put forth one or more yearly of the poorest children born within the town of Ulverstone, excluding such as are born within the hamlet or elsewhere, save only those that are born within the precincts of the said town. I likewise give and bequeath thirty pounds, the interest whereof yearly is to go towards the maintenance of a school master, to be kept at Ulverstone, for the teaching of poor children, which sum of thirty pounds my executors are to pay within one year after my decease, to such persons as will give unto them good security for answering yearly the interest thereof, to the end and purpose aforesaid. Item. I give and bequeath twenty pounds unto Mary Arkewe, for her faithful and careful service performed unto my wife and children in all their extremities. I give and bequeath unto Joseph Sharpe, my faithful and careful servant at the Marsh Grange, fifty shillings, and the like sum unto Ann Jaykes who hath approved herself a very honest and careful servant ever since she came to the Marsh. I do hereby likewise give and bequeath unto my dear, careful and entirely beloved

Margaret Fell, my wife, fifty pounds as a token and testimony of my dearest affection unto her. I likewise give unto James Fell, twenty shillings to buy him a ring therewith as a token of my love unto him.

* * * * *

As to my executors who are to have no other benefit nor advantage by this my will and testament than is hereafter expressed; that is to say, I give to each of them five pounds apiece, for the cares and pains they are to undergo in the discharge of trust hereby imposed on them. * * * * *

I do hereby revoke and make void all wills and testaments by me made, and I do hereby give unto my beloved son, George Fell, as many of my law-books as will make those which he hath the complete body of the law, and wherein they shall prove defective, my executors shall sell so many of the rest of my law books as will buy those that are wanting. I do hereby in further token of my love and affection for my dear wife, give and bequeath unto her, my dwelling house, onsett, with all the buildings, stables, barns, orchards, gardens, therewith, all used and occupied, with fifty acres of ground, lying most conveniently unto the said house, and to be set out and divided by my executors. * * * * *

And lastly I do publish and declare this to be my last will and testament. In witness whereof I have hereunto set my hand and seal, the day and year first above written.

THOMAS FELL.

Witness hereof, GEO. FELL,
    THOS. GRAMES,
    THOMAS KNYPE,
    WM. BENSON.

This will was proved at London the 4th day of December, 1658, by the oath of the executors, to whom was committed administration.

The discovery of the foregoing will places before us a document peculiarly characteristic of Judge Fell. With approach of death, as in life, he kindly remembered his servants, also the aged poor and the children of the poor. The value of these small bequests in that day can better be understood by taking into account the wages common at that time. A laboring man got from three half-pence to two pence per day. A woman a penny a day, often less. Five pounds then would probably have purchased to the value of twenty-five pounds at the present day.

Margaret Fell had a settlement independent of what is mentioned in the will. It was an annuity payable from the Hawkswell estate, which estate went, by inheritance to their son George Fell. Being heir to that family property he is not mentioned as a legatee in his father's will except in connection with a set of law books.

Swarthmoor must have been purchased by Judge Fell or his father. It could not have been an entailed estate since it was divided between Margaret Fell and her daughters. One-third of the Marsh Grange also belonged to the widow of Judge Fell, so that she was left in good circumstances. She remained at Swarthmoor Hall for the next 11 years dispensing a generous hospitality and making many journeys to London and throughout the Kingdom, speaking in the Friends' meeting houses and appearing before magistrates and frequently before the King in behalf of the persecuted Friends or Quakers. In 1669 Margaret Fell was married to George Fox, the founder of the Society of Friends. The marriage certificate has been preserved and the following is an exact copy of that document:

MARRIAGE CERTIFICATE OF GEORGE FOX AND MARGARET FOX IN
1669.

"These are to signify unto all whom this may concern, that on the eighteenth day of the Eighth month, in the year one thousand six hundred and sixty-nine, George Fox and Margaret Fell propounded their intentions of joining together in honorable marriage, in the covenant of God, in our men's meeting at Broad Meade, in the City of Bristol, (having before made mention of such their intentions to several friends,) on the behalf of which there were several testimonies given, both by the children and relations of the said Margaret, then present, and several others, in the power of the Lord, both of men and women, declaring their satisfaction and approbation of their declared intention of marriage. And, likewise, at another meeting both of men and women, at the place aforesaid, on the 21st day of the year and month aforesaid, the said George Fox and Margaret Fell did again publish their intentions of joining together in the honorable marriage, in the covenant of God, unto which again there were many living testimonies borne by relations and friends, then present, both of men and women. And the said intentions were again published by Dennis Hollister at our public meeting, place aforesaid, on the two and twentieth day of the year and month aforesaid; and then again a public testimony was given to the same, that it was of God, who had brought it to pass, and for the full accomplishment of the aforesaid and approved intention, at a public meeting, both of men and women friends appointed on purpose for the same thing, at the place aforesaid, and on the twenty-seventh day of the year and month aforesaid, according to the law and ordinance of God, and the example and good order of his people, mentioned in the Scriptures of truth, who took each other before witnesses and the Elders of the people, as Laban appointed a meeting at the marriage of Jacob and as a meeting was appointed on purpose when Boaz and Ruth took each other, and also as it was in Cana, where Christ and his disciples went to a marriage, the said George Fox did solemnly in the presence of God and us, his people, declare that he took the said Margaret Fell, in the everlasting power and covenant of God, which is from everlasting to everlasting; and in the honorable marriage to be his bride and wife. And, likewise, the said Margaret did solemnly declare that in the everlasting power of the mighty God, and in the unalterable word, and in the presence of God, his angels and us, His Holy assembly, she took the said George Fox to be her husband, unto which marriage many living testimonies were borne, in a sense of the power and presence of the living God, manifested in the said assembly, of which we, whose names are here subscribed, are witnesses:"

"John Rous,	Margaret Rous,
Wm. Yeamans,	Isabell Yeamans,
Thos. Lower,	Mary Lower,
Geo. Roberts,	Sarah Fell,
Geo. Whitehead,	Susan Fell,
Thos. Salthouse,	Rachel Fell,
Robt. Widder,	Ann Whitehead,
Leonard Fell,	Margaret Besse,
Morgan Watkins,	Susannah Pearson,
	Mary Wakefield,"

and many other men and women Friends.

It will be seen that the whole public proceedings from the date of publication, from first to last, occupied only nine days; and that neither husband nor wife signed the certificate. This marriage certificate is one of the earliest of its kind that has been preserved and is interesting as being that of the "Father and Mother of the Society of Friends." Margaret and George Fox lived happily together for a period of eleven years, or till the death of George Fox, which occurred in January 1691. Margaret Fox received the news of her husband's death in the following letter written by Wm. Penn.

"London 13" of 11th Mo. 1690. (Jan. 1691).

"Dear M. Fox:—With the precious remembrance of thy unfeigned love in Jesus Christ, I am to be the teller to thee of sorrowful tidings, which are these: that thy dear husband and my beloved friend George Fox, finished his glorious testimony this night about half an hour after nine o'clock, being sensible till the last breath. Oh, he is gone and has left us with a storm over our heads. Surely in great mercy to him, but an evidence to us of sorrows coming. He was as lively and as firm as ever on Fourth-day, was a week at Grace Church Street; and also the last First-day, being the day before yesterday. But he complained after meeting of being inwardly struck

—44—

and lay down at Henry Goldney's where his spirit departed. My soul is deeply afflicted with this sudden great loss. Surely it portends to us evils to come. A prince indeed is fallen in Israel today May the Lord be with thee and thine, and with us all. Amen.

I am thy faithful and affectionate friend,

WILLIAM PENN."

Robert Barrow, in a letter to Henry Coward and some other Lancaster friends says, "Our ancient friend and elder in the church George Fox, was this day buried in the presence of a large assembly, of God's people, supposed to be about 4000 friends. The meeting house at Grace Church Street could not contain them; nor the court before the door." George Fox was interred in Bunhill Fields' burying ground in the heart of the city of London. The writer has visited his grave twice in recent years and has found it somewhat difficult to locate the spot. A street has been cut through the old burying grounds and on one side is now the "Dissenters Ground," where are buried Susannah Wesley, the mother of John and Charles Wesley, Isaac Watts, John Bunyan, Daniel DeFoe and many other eminent personages. The grave of George Fox is on the other side of the new street and seems to be the only one in that vicinity, at least the only one marked. A simple slab, some 15 inches high, bears the name and the dates of his birth and death, (1624-1691.) The will of George Fox, leaving all his books and papers in the care of our ancestors, William and Sarah Meade, is here copied.

THE WILL OF GEORGE FOX.

Proved 30th December, 1697. Extract from the records of the Prerogative Court of Canterbury.

"I do give to Thomas Lower my saddle and bridle and spurs, and boots (inward leathered) and the New England Indian Bible and my great book of the signifying of names, and my book of the New Testament of eight languages and all my physical things that came from beyond the seas, with the outlandish cup and my two dials, the one is an equinoctial dial. And all my overplus books to be divided between my four sons-in-law, and also all my other books and my hammock, I do give to Thomas Lower; they are in Benjamin Antrobus' chest; and Rachel may take that which is at Swarthmoore. And Thomas Lower may have my walnut equinoctial dial (and if he can, may get one cut by it, which will be hard to do), and he shall have one of my prospect glasses in my trunk at London, and a pair of my gloves and my seal, G. F. The flaming sword to Nat Mead, and my other two seals to J. Rous and Dan Abraham. And Thomas Lower shall have my magnifying glass and the tortoise shell comb and case.

And all that I have written concerning what I do give to my relations; either money or otherwise, John Loft may put it up in my trunk at John Elsone's and write all things down in a paper and make a paper out of all my papers, how I have ordered things for them. And John Loft may send all things down by Poulesworth carrier, in the trunk, to John Fox, at Poulesworth, in Warwickshire, and let John Fox send John Loft a full receipt and a discharge; and in this matter none of you may be concerned but John Loft. And my other little trunk that standeth in Benjamin Antrobus' closet, with the outlandish things, Thomas Lower shall have; and if it be ordered in any other papers, to any other, that must not stand so, but as now ordered, G. F. And Sary, thou may give Sary Frickenfield half a guinea, for she hath been serviceable to me, an honest, careful young woman, G. F. Make no noise of these things, but do them in the life as I have ordered them.

And let Thomas Dockeral, that knoweth many of my epistles and written books, which he did write (copy) come up to London to assist friends in sorting of my epistles and other writings, give him a guinea, G. F. And when all is done and cleared, what remains to go to the printing of my books. Benjamin Antrobus and Mary have 100 pounds of mine—take no use of them (interest) for it when you receive it. And in my chest, in Benj. Antrobus' chamber, there is a little gilt box with some gold in it; Sary Mead to take it, and let it do its services among the rest, so far as it will go; the box is sealed up—G. F.

I do order William and Sary Mead and T. Lower, to take care of all my books and epistles and papers that be at Benjamin Antrobus' and R. R. Chambers', and those that come from Swarthmore, and my journal of my life, and the passages and travels of friends, and to take them all in their hands, and all the overplus of them they may have and keep together as a library, when they have gathered them together that are to be printed. And for them to take charge of all my money and defray all as I have ordered in my other papers and anything more of mine they may take, and God will and shall be their reward,—the 8th month, 1688.

And all the passages and travels and sufferings of friends, in the beginning of the spreading of the truth, which I have kept together, will make a fine history, and they may be had at Swarthmore with my other books. Glory to the Lord forever. Amen. G. F.—the 8th month, 1688."

"The persons hereinafter named, by their solemn declaration, subscribed under their hands, did affirm the above written to be wrote with the proper hand of the said George Fox, deceased, they being acquainted with his handwriting:—"

"S. Mead, wife of W. Mead, of the parish of St. Dyonis, Back-church, London, citizen of London.

W. Ingram, of the parish of St. Margaret, London, aged about 57 years; he knew George Fox about 40 years.

G. Whitehead, of the parish of St. Botolph, London, gentleman, aged about 60 years; knew Geo. Fox above 40 years."

The spelling of proper names in the foregoing will and certificate is left as in the original.

Those who are acquainted with the common written document of the seventeenth century, will be aware how uncertain is their spelling of proper names, different members of the same family not unfrequently spelling their own names and the name of the family residence differently. Thus we find Swarthmoor sometimes spelled Swarthmore, Swartmore, Swarthmoar and Swartmoar; and William and Sarah Meade's name which they always terminated with an *e*, has no such termination in the above will. The descendants of William and Sarah Meade who came to America, seem to have dropped this terminal *e* and the name in our family, has for several generations, been spelled *Mead*.

Margaret Fox survived her second husband for eleven years and in her old age was particularly active in her works of charity and in her preaching amongst the early Friends. At various times she was fined and imprisoned. At one time she was confined for over three years in Lancaster jail. In Devonshire House, London, is a collection of manuscripts which contains over four hundred letters of the various members of the Fell family. Margaret Fox was personally acquainted and had interviews with Charles I., Oliver Cromwell, Charles II, James II, William III and Queen Mary, and with Anne, afterwards Queen. To these monarchs she frequently sent letters and petitions, and these or copies thereof are on file in the Devonshire House collection. We will here give copies of two very remarkable productions written by our ancestress in her extreme age.

TO KING WILLIAM.

"It hath pleased Almighty God to bring me unto this place, (London) two hundred miles from my outward dwelling, in my old age, (being entered into my 85th year) to bear testimony for that eternal Truth which I and many more are made partakers of, praised be the Lord. But I am not free to return to my habitation until I have cleared myself to this government. I was exercised in this manner the first year King Charles II came to the crown, and laboured among them (at court) a whole year to acquaint them with our principles. Great opposition we had, both from Church and State, yet it

—47—

pleased God to cause them to give us some liberty to worship Him, though sometimes under great sufferings.

"And now I am to acquaint King William that we have been a people for about forty-six years, having lived under several reigns, and we have suffered very much, as is well known to the nation of England, even to the death of several hundreds by imprisonment and other hardships. Yet we were never found in the transgression of any just or righteous law, but only suffered upon account of our consciences towards God.

"We do deny and condemn all plotting and contriving against the government, and all false underhand dealing. We live in the maintenance of that principle which is righteous, just and true; for God is a God of Truth and blessed are all they that fear Him and walk in His Truth.

"And now God has placed thee over us in this Government, who hast been very moderate and merciful to us, and we live very comfortably under thee, and do enjoy our meetings quietly. God has blessed thy Government and prospered thy undertakings, for which the King and we have cause to bless His Holy name, who is the God of Peace, and His Son, the Prince of Peace, who has given us tranquility.

Thy gentle government and clemency and gracious acts, God hath and will reward thee for. And as we abide in the just and righteous principles of God, I hope the Government shall never hear worse of us, but that we shall rather be a blessing than grievance to it and the nation. So it will be if we continue in the blessed Truth, in which I pray God for thy preservation, who am His servant and thy faithful subject." MARGARET FOX.

"London, 24th of 4th month, called June, 1698."

The second document is a most remarkable one; not only is it the last from Margaret Fox's pen, but its declarations and tone show that though at such an advanced age, her mental and spiritual energies were still bright and vigorous. This epistle, or testimony of Margaret Fox's, was written by her when in the 88th year of her age and only a few months prior to her death.

MARGARET FOX'S REVIVAL OF HER TESTIMONY.

"To God Almighty I appeal, whom I serve with my spirit in the Gospel of His Son, whose I am, and to whom I am given up with mine heart and soul to serve, who hath been my Father and leader ever since I knew Him, who hath led me through many trials and sufferings and exercises that were a cross to flesh and blood; who hath upheld and supported me therein down to this day. And now in mine old age (88 years old), I am forced to renew my testimony again, through a false, lying spirit gotten up amongst us to oppose and withstand our gracious, blessed Truth, in the which we are begotten, and in the which we who are preserved out of this Spirit do stand in that blessed Unity of the Eternal Spirit, which joineth us to the Lord, and one to another. But an imaginary, false and untrue spirit, hath gotten into some, by which they are deluded and will not see or apprehend by any means used to give them satisfaction. Yet for the satisfaction of friends and others I give this, my testimony, while I breathe upon the earth, that I shall stand for God and Truth.

He hath taught me to render to all men what is their due, and not to owe anything to any but love. In that which is righteous and just, God hath taught us and manifested His will. And He commands that we should render to Caesar the things that are Caesar's and to God the things that are God's; which I shall by His holy assistance and power endeavor to fulfill both to God and man. This I am moved of the Lord to acquaint all with, whilst I have breath and being upon the earth.

Given under my hand this 24th day of the 9th month, Anno Domino, 1701."

MARGARET FOX."

The closing scene was not far distant when the above was written. As her last moments drew near, she asked her beloved daughter, Rachel, to take her in her arms, and then saying, "I am at peace," gently breathed her last.

Thus lived and died the great-grand-daughter of Anne Askew, the martyr. She died on the 23rd day of the 2nd month (O. S.), 1702, in the 88th year of her age. Her remains were interred in the Friends' burial ground belonging to Swarthmoor Meeting House, at Sunbreck, on the 27th day of the same month; the burial being attended by a great concourse of Friends from several counties, and of the neighboring, gentry and peasantry.

CHAPTER VIII.

DESCENDANTS OF THOMAS AND MARGARET FELL.

19TH GENERATION.—Thomas Fell, M. P., born 1598, died 1658, married Margaret Askew in 1631. Margaret Askew was born in 1613, died Feb. 23rd, 1702. They had issue,

20TH GENERATION.—(1st.) Margaret, married John Rous in 1661 and died in 1706, aged 63. Has no living descendants.

(2nd.) Bridget, married John Draper, 1662. Left no children. No record of her death has been discovered.

(3rd.) George Fell, only son, married in 1668, but wife's name not known. Died between 1670 and 73, leaving two children: a son named CHARLES and a daughter ISABELLA, who was married to James Graves, but of her descendants nothing is known. Charles on coming of age sold the Hawkswell estate to his Uncle Daniel Abraham. Charles Fell's son CHARLES married Gulielma Maria Penn, grand-daughter of William Penn. *Their only child* was Robert Edward Fell, who is supposed to have died unmarried, and thus Robert Edward was the last in descent through the male line from the Fells of Swarthmoor, Hall.

(4th.) Isabel, married William Yeamans, a Bristol merchant son of Robert Yeamans, Sheriff of Bristol, who was hanged for his loyal politics, at his father-in-law's door, early in the civil war. Wm. Yeamans died in 1674. Their last son *William*, died at his Uncle Meade's in Essex, in 1697, aged 28. Isabel married a second time in 1689, to Abraham Morrice, of Lincoln. She died in 1704. Her husband in 1705.

(5th.) SARAH, the fourth daughter, married WILLIAM MEADE in 1681, she died in 1714, at Gooseyes, in Essex, aged 71. William Meade died in 1713 aged 89. William and Sarah being our ancestors in the direct line (Generation 20) will receive further notice.

(6th.) Mary, the 5th daughter, married Thos. Lower, M. D., in 1668, and died in 1719, aged seventy five years. Thomas Lower died in 1720, aged eighty-eight. They had 10 children, but only 5 of them lived to maturity. These were, 1st *Margery*, born 1675, married Benjamin Robinson, in 1700. 2nd, *Loveday*,

born 1677, married to William Swan, in 1690. 3rd, *Mary*, born
1678, married to William Arch in 1701. 4th, *Richard*, born 1682,
died 1705. 5th, *Bridget*, born 1688, married to Evan Ward, of
London. There are but one or two descendants of Mary and
Thomas Lower living at the present writing.

(7th.) Susanna, the sixth daughter, married William Ingram,
left no children, date of her death unknown. She was living in
1706, at time of her husband's death.

(8th.) Rachel, the seventh daughter, born 1653, married
Daniel Abraham, 1682, died 1732, aged 79. Daniel died 1731,
aged 69. They left but one child, John Abraham, born 1687,
who died in 1771, aged 84 years, leaving a numerous posterity.
This *John Abraham* sold Swarthmoor Hall, in 1759 and removed
to Seaton, near Lancaster.

We will now return to our ancestors William and Sarah Meade, or
Mead, (20th Generation.) Wm. Meade is first mentioned by George
Fox in 1670, on the occasion of his and William Penn's arrest and
imprisonment. He is then spoken of as one who had recently joined
the Friends. He belonged to a family in Essex, of considerable
landed property and influence. He had a house in London as well
as a country residence. On the occasion of his proving the handwriting of George Fox in his will, he is styled "citizen and mer-
chant-tailor," but that is understood to have reference merely to the
city guild of which he was a member. The estate of Gooseyes, situated near Romford, in Essex, was purchased by William Meade from
Lord Dudley and Ward, about the year 1670. Gooseyes is a Manor
in the living of Havering, and the house belonging to it being rebuilt
by Lord Dudley was formerly a mansion of considerable importance,
but most of it has now been torn down. The meeting house and
burial ground at Barking, about six miles from Gooseyes was on land
that belonged to the Meades, and the title of the leassee was purchased by Friends in 1672 and the meeting house erected at Wm.
Meade's expense. In further evidence of the importance and hold-
ings of the Meade family I searched the Essex and Yorkshire records
and have found the following entries concerning Thomas Meade,
(Generation 19,) the father of Wm. Meade. "15th of Jas. I, (1618)
Thomas Meade, gentleman, gave 75 shillings for license to concord
with Philip, Lord Wharton, Knight, touching six messuages, six cot-
tages, 2 mills, 12 gardens, 100 acres of arable land, 400 acres of
meadow, 600 acres of pasture, 2000 acres of juniper and briar,
and 10 pounds rents, with all the appurtenances in Helaugh, Grinton
and Swaledale and half the manors of Swaledale and Grinton."

"4th of Charles I, (1628.) Indenture made between Thomas
Meade, gentleman and Sir Thomas Vachell, Knight, touching half

the manors of Helaugh and Swaledale and divers other lands in Swaledale and Grinton."

"4th of Charles I. Indenture between same, sale by Thomas Meade to Sir Thomas Vachell of half the manors of Helaugh and Swaledale and *Swandale* and lands in Grinton "

"4th of Charles I. Sir Thomas Vachell, Knight, gave the King 60 shillings for license to concord with Thos. Meade and *Johanna* his wife, three messuages, three collages, 1 water-mill, 6 gardens, 50 acres of arable land, 200 acres of meadow land, 300 acres of pasture, 1000 acres of juniper and briar, and 10 pounds rents, with the appurtenances, in Helaugh, Grinton and Swaledale."

(GENERATION 21.)—Nathaniel Meade, only son of William and Sarah Meade, not being satisfied with the life of a country gentleman, and wishing to study for the law, entered the Middle Temple as a student, as is shown by the following record: -"August 13th, 1700, Mr. Nathaniel Meade, son and heir apparent of William Meade, of Gooseyes, in the county of Essex, Esq., was admitted into the Society of the Middle Temple, and is especially bound up in company with it, and gives by fine four pounds." At that date he was sixteen years old. At his father's death in 1713, he was 29 and a rising Barrister, possessed of considerable talent. After his mother's death in 1714, he erected a vault in the centre of the Friends' burying ground at Barking, where the remains of his parents were laid side by side, and a plain headstone placed, with the following inscription:

"Here lyeth the Body of William Meade, Esq.,
Who departed this life the 3rd day of April,
1713 in the 86th year of his age.
And also Mrs. Sarah Meade
Who died the 9th of June, 1714, in
The 71st year of her age."

After his parents' death Nathaniel Meade pursued his profession successfully, became Sergeant-at-Law, eventually was knighted by King George II, and died in 1760. He was the intimate friend, in his youth, of William Penn, and there were family connections that made the friendship stronger. His death is recorded in the "London Chronicle" (in the British Museum) of April 17th-19th—1760.

"On Tuesday morning last, died at his house in Litchfield Street, near Newport Market, very much advanced in years, SIR NATHANIEL MEADE, KNIGHT, a gentleman universally respected." It is believed that all of Sir Nathaniel Meade's children came to America. One of them is buried close to the grave of Benjamin Franklin in Philadelphia.

CHAPTER IX.

Of the wife of Sir Nathaniel Mead we have no account, but of his children we have the names of William, John, Samuel and Robert. It is not certain that this is the proper order of their ages, but we find that they came to Bucks Co., Pa., early in the 18th century, and that our ancestor WILLIAM MEAD married ELLEN WORRALL, daughter of Thomas and Mary Worrall of Cheshire, England. Ellen Worrall had two sisters: Elizabeth, who married Joseph Warder, and Martha who married George Brown.

William Mead and Ellen Worrall were married in the year, 1719 and removed from Bucks Co., Pa. to Virginia, in 1745. William Mead died in 1784, and his will is recorded in the records of Leesburg, Loudoun County, on Aug. 9th., 1784. (Written Jan. 17th, 1780.) He was about 90 years of age at the time of his death. In his will he mentions his two grandsons, William Wright and Joseph Wright and the three children of Hannah Thomas,* viz., Martha, Mary and Thomas Thomas.

William and Ellen Mead had six children, of whom Hannah was the oldest, born in 1720. The second child, Mary, married a Rhodes and after his death, a Brown.

The third daughter, Anne Mead, married Abram Mason, the fourth daughter, Martha, married a Wright; the fifth daughter, Elizabeth, married Ezekiel Potts. The sixth child and only son, William Mead, was born in 1736, married Mary Shreve, in Virginia, 1785, and died in 1816, aged 80 years. A remarkable fact in his history is that he married at 49 years of age, had two children, and his son, Thomas Meade also married at 49 and had two children Henry and Elizabeth. This daughter, Mrs. Elizabeth Meade-Hoffecker, of Wilmington, Delaware, is still living and a young woman—the only representative in her line, of the *third generation*, where ordinarily there would have been *six generations* if early marriages had prevailed.

HANNAH MEAD, the oldest child of William and Ellen Mead, married Capt. John Thomas of Bowie's Island, in the Potomac river,

---

*Hannah Meade's cousins, the daughters of Col. David Meade of Chaumiere, Ky., who had removed from the estate of Maycox, Prince George County, Va., opposite Westover, married three of the most useful and eminent men of Ohio. These were Nathaniel Massie, the founder of the city of Chillicothe and once elected Governor of Ohio, who married Susan Meade; Charles Wyllings Byrd, Sec'y of the Northwestern Territory and Acting Governor of Ohio, member of the Constitutional Convention of 1802, who married Sarah Meade; and Dr. William Creighton, Junior the first Secretary of state of the state of Ohio and twice a member of Congress who married a third sister.

near Leesburg, Loudoun Co., Va. She was his second wife, he having been previously married to a Mrs. Harrison Taylor, the owner of the Island. Captain John Thomas was born in London, England, probably as early as the year 1698, for he first appears in the records of Loudoun County, in 1748 and was then about 50 years old. His father, John Thomas, afterwards Bishop of Rochester, who died in 1774, had purchased for him a commission in the British Army, but coming early to America he soon forsook the King's service and after Braddock's defeat, in which action he was a participant, he became a captain in the Virginia Line and served his adopted country throughout the Revolutionary war. His commission has been preserved in the family and there are those still living who distinctly remember to have seen it and also his sword, but it is not known where these valuable family relics are at present preserved. The state of Virginia did tardy justice to the old man, who survived almost all his comrades of the early French and Indian wars and lived a life of ease and quiet in Leesburg until almost 100 years old. It was not until after his death that his heirs were granted a tract of 4,000 acres of land by way of recompense for the long continued military service of their father.

The following certified copy of the records of the Virginia Land office will be available as proof in case any of the John Thomas descendants wish to join the Sons or Daughters of the Revolution.

"No. 6755. In Council, Nov. 2nd, 1830.

It is advised that John Thomas be allowed land bounty as a Captain in the Continental line for service during the War.

JOHN FLOYD,
Governor of Virginia.

Attest:

J. W. PLEASANTS.

A warrant for 4000 acres issued to John Thomas, No. 6755, Nov. 3rd, 1830, and delivered to Col. John Nicholas.
Land Office, Richmond, Va.

I hereby certify that the foregoing is a true copy of the records of this office. Witness my hand and seal of office, this 7th day of January, 1901.

{ Seal. }   JOHN W. RICHARDSON,

Register of the Land Office."

Captain Thomas, by his second wife Hannah Mead, was the father of three children whom he mentioned in his will as Martha Jackson, Mary Hole and Thomas Thomas. This will is on record in

Loudoun Co., and was signed by John Thomas, Sept. 15, 1791. He was a celebrated *bon-vivant* and "a jolly good fellow" about town until a very advanced age, for the writer has seen various records of fines of 5 pounds and 10 pounds—imposed against said John Thomas and two or three of his convivial companions, for "playing at cards" and "gambling," at certain tap-rooms and taverns in the ancient city of Leesburg as late as the year 1790, when he was certainly past 90 years old.

His wife Hannah died soon after the close of the Revolutionary War—Of his daughter, Martha Jackson, we have no further record and it is not thought that she left any posterity. Of the other children, Mary Hole and Thomas Thomas, more will be said after speaking here of the other members of the Mead family.

William Mead, only brother of our great-great-grandmother Hannah Mead Thomas, married, as before stated, in 1785, Mary Shreve, in Loudoun Co., Virginia. He was born in Bucks Co., Pa., in 1736. His parents removed from the Township of Lower Wakefield in 1745, obtaining a certificate of removal from Falls Monthly Meeting of Friends. This certificate is now on record in the Penn. Historical Society rooms. They removed to Fairfax Co., Virginia, and lived there until a few years before his death when he removed, with his family, to Loudoun Co. (As Loudoun County was erected from Fairfax it may be that William Mead's lands were in what afterwards became Loudoun Co.) At time of his death he also owned lands in Bedford County. (This was *William Mead Sr.*, son of Sir Nathaniel Mead of England, and now a very aged man.)

The old Mead homestead in Loudoun Co., Va., is still standing and has been visited by the writer. It is called "Greenway" and is situated one and one-half miles from Leesburg on the Aldie Pike. Joseph Mead added to the old house and occupied it until his death in 1870. This estate is beautifully situated and the manor house is well preserved. The Southern and Northern armies encamped on the estate during the civil war but the buildings escaped destruction. William Mead and Mary Shreve his wife had a large family which we will enumerate briefly.

1. William Mead, born 1786, married Mary Winston Crenshaw, of Bedford Co., Va. Had four children. Died in Bedford 1854.

2. Ellen Mead, died an infant.

3. Ellen Mead 2nd, born 1789, married Robert Moffett; lived and died in Loudoun Co., Va. Had three daughters.

4. Elizabeth Mead, died 1818.

5. Ann Mead, married Elias Schooley, left one son Fenton Schooley, also deceased. Ann was born 1794—died 1857.

6. Mary Mead, born 1797, died 1859, married T. Saunders; had

three daughters, two sons. (Thomas was a Major in U. S. army) one of these sons now living.*

7. Joseph Mead, married Jane Worsley; born 1799, died 1870. Had two sons and two daughters.

8. Thomas Mead, married Mary Worsley; lived in Bedford Co., Va. Was county surveyor and a highly educated man. Was writing a history of the Mead family at the time of his sudden death and papers were destroyed.

9. Martha Mead, married Frederick Carper of Fairfax County, Va., died in Fairfax County in 1876. Left two sons and two daughters.

We now return to the remaining children of Captain John Thomas, Mary Hole and Thomas Thomas. This brother and sister left a numerous posterity and their descendants have always been associated together and intermarried until at the present time there are curious relationships and common descendants in both lines. Mary, who was born in 1757, married Jacob Hole (generation XXVIII) and is the ancestress of all that numerous family of Holes descended from the eleven children of this marriage. Her line with that of Jacob, her husband, will be noticed later.

Her younger brother, "Thomas Thomas, born in 1759, enlisted September 22nd, 1777, and served one month as private in Captain Joseph Paucoast's Company, First Regiment, Burlington Co., New Jersey Militia. Served one month during the year 1777 as private in Captain Joseph Vandyke's Company, First Regiment, Burlington Co., New Jersey Militia. Served one month during 1777 as private in Captain Joseph Weaver's Company, 2nd Regiment, Burlington Co., New Jersey Militia. Served 12 days during June, 1778, as private in Captain Edward G. Thomas' Company, 1st Regiment, Burlington Co. Militia.

Served one month as private in Captain Marmaduke Curtis' Company, 2nd Regiment, Burlington Co., N. J. Militia. Served two years as private in Captain Richard Shreve's Troop of Light Horse, Burlington Co., N. J. Militia.

Enlisted January 15th, 1778, and served a month as private in Captain Jacob Perkins' Company, Burlington Co., N. J. Militia. Served one month as private in Captain Zachariah Clevenger's Company, 1st Regiment, Burlington Co., N. J. Militia, during the Revolutionary War." This war record of Thomas Thomas is given

*This son, Adj't. Gen. John S. Sauders, died Jan. 19, 1904, since this book went to press.) He died at the home of his daughter Mrs. Bullard, wife of Lieut. Commander W. H. J. Bullard of the Naval Academy. He was 68 years old, graduated from West Point in 185x. Entered the Confederate army and became assistant inspector general. Later he was appointed assistant ordinance officer of the army of Northern Virginia. General Saunders, when Lieutenant in the U. S. army, was one of those detailed to escort the Prince of Wales, now King Edward VII, during his visit to this country in 1860.

under the seal of the Adjutant General of N. J. Signed, "William S. Stryker, Adjutant General, N. J., August 3, 1900."

The above named and oft-enlisted Thomas Thomas, married Mary Grimes, in New Jersey or after returning to Virginia, it is not known where or when. Their daughter, Margaret Thomas, an only child, married Edward Morton. Margaret was born in Westmoreland Co., Pa., in 1794 and died in 1829. Margaret and Edward Morton came into Ohio in 1821. Previous to that time they had lived in Virginia. Soon after their marriage Edward was drafted for service in the war of 1812 but hired a substitute. He was born Jan. 15, 1790, and died Oct. 10, 1834. Both he and his wife, Margaret, are buried at Fletcher Church, in Guernsey Co. Ohio.

Edward Morton was the son of Moses Morton who came to the United States at the age of 7 years and died in 1821, aged 62 years. His wife Mary Dowler, died in 1826 and both are buried at Bellville, Pa. Edward and Margaret Morton have one child still living in the person of Moses Thomas Morton, of Barnesville, Ohio, now in his 87th year. Moses T. Morton, born November 23rd, 1817, married Mary Cooper, of Washington County, Pa., daughter of Lemuel Cooper, (born 1795, died 1882), and Mary Morton, (daughter of Moses Morton and Mary Dowler.) They celebrated their golden wedding August 26th, 1891, at which time all their children and grandchildren were present, there never having been a death in the family. Mrs. Mary (Cooper) Morton died on her 73rd anniversary, July 14, 1895.

To Moses T. and Mary C. Morton were born four children: Jennie, who married William Wilkin and lives in Delaware, Ohio; Melissa, who married John W. Rose and lives at Fairview, Ohio; Rev. John T. a member of the East Ohio M. E. Conference and now pastor of Willson Ave. M. E. Church, Cleveland, Ohio, married Mollie Cowgill of Fairview, Ohio; and E. Cooper Morton who married Sept. 30, 1869, Sarah Ellen Holtz, daughter of Jacob Holtz and Sarah Eleanor Douglas, of Fairview, Ohio. Here are some singular coincidents: The Earls of Morton are Douglases. The family name being interchangeable, some bearing the name of Morton and some of Douglas. In the Hole family the name of Eleanor Douglas occurs a number of times in the English branch. As the Holes and Douglases are so mixed and intermarried, the Douglas genealogy will be completely given in Appendix A, and the portrait of the oldest living representative of that noble family, Mrs. Sarah Eleanor (Douglas) Holtz, in her 92nd year—will be found on page 58. Sarah Eleanor Douglas was born Sept. 4, 1812, married Jacob Holtz Dec. 30, 1830, and lived to celebrate with him their 69th wedding anniversary. Jacob Holtz died Feb. 2nd, 1900, at the age of 93 years. His grandmother Holtz died in Morristown, Ohio, at the age of 103 years. Mrs. Sarah E. Holtz's mother, Rebecca Douglas, died aged 92 years—this much in the interests of longevity.

To return to the family of E. Cooper Morton, we learn that his five children are the grand children of Sarah Eleanor Douglas Holtz and the great great grandchildren of Thomas Thomas, the brother of Mary Hole. Herman Norville Morton, the eldest son, married, Dec. 24, 1897, Virginia A. Rice, who is a great grand daughter of Mary Hole, and also a descendant of the Douglases of England. They have one son, Charles Theodore Morton, born in Sandusky, Ohio. Prof. H. N. Morton is now Principal of the Urbana, O., High School.

Rev. Emmett Wilkin Morton, the second son of E. Cooper Morton, married Winifred, daughter of the Rev. T. P. Marsh, D. D., President of Mount Union College, and of Harriet Newhall, his wife, who is a descendant of Deacon Elmund Rice, the pilgrim, and a common ancestor of the English Rices in the U. S. Rev. E. W. Morton is pastor of the M. E. Church at Chautauqua, N. Y.

The third son of E. Cooper Morton, Ira Abbott Morton, was graduated in the Classical course, from Mt. Union College in 1903 (as were his brothers H. N. and E. W. in 1896 and 1897) and is now a divinity student at Drew Theological Seminary, Madison, N. J.

Ellen O. Morton, and Mary Louisa Morton, the two daughters of E. C. Morton reside at home in Barnesville, Ohio. Another son E. D. Holtz Morton, died in infancy, May 23d, 1875.

Mrs. Sarah Holtz Morton, wife of E. Cooper Morton, died March 16, 1893. Mr. Morton married Miss Mary Susan Anderson, Sept. 29th, 1895, and they now reside in Barnesville, O.

Moses T. Morton, whose portrait is presented in this volume, resides with them.

CHAPTER X.

[Excepting the descendants of their son, Charles, whose line will be traced in the next chapter.]

In the year 1740, JACOB HOLE, a grandson of the Rev. Thomas Hole, of Caunton, Nottinghamshire, England, emigrated to Pennsylvania, with his family of grown up sons. Settling in Bucks County, the parents spent the remainder of their days there and were buried in that county. The record of their death has not been discovered. Three of the sons removed from Bucks County, Pa., to Virginia. These were Peter, Charles and Daniel.

JOHN HOLE, the fourth son, (probably the 2nd by birth) settled in New York state and we know nothing of his descendants except that Judge Joseph Holt, afterwards of Kentucky, (Secretary of War and Postmaster General of the U. S.) claimed relationship with the Virginia Holes through the line of John Hole, who had changed the spelling of the name. The Hon. Joseph Holt was a grandson of John Hole and he was the only descendant known.

PETER HOLE, the oldest son of Jacob, said to be a half-brother to the others, never married. He died in Loudoun County, Virginia, and was buried at Lincoln, (then called Goose Creek Meeting) in the ancient burying ground where George Fox had preached when on his visit to the colonies. Peter Hole must have been considerably over 100 years of age at the time of his death, which occurred about the year 1825. He could not have been born later than the year 1717 and would be 108 years old in 1825.

CHARLES HOLE, the third son of Jacob Hole, was born in 1728, and was 12 years old when he came to America. He married in Pennsylvania but removed to Loudoun County, Virginia, in 1758. He died in 1812, aged 76 years. He left a large family and his line will be traced fully in another chapter.

DANIEL HOLE, the fourth son of Jacob Hole, was born in 1730, died 1814. That he moved to Virginia at an early date is shown by a letter from his grandson, Daniel Hole, of Versailles, Darke Co., O., written in 1888, when he was in his eighty-third year. "My grandfather, Daniel Hole, emigrated from England and settled in Virginia. He had four sons, Zachariah, John, William and Daniel. William was the father of the writer. He moved to Kentucky at an early day; settled near Lexington. From there he moved to Fort Washington, now Cincinnati; lived there five years. Moved forty miles north and settled close to where Miamisburg now stands and died there."

A letter from Joseph Hole, written Aug. 12, 1888, from Drakesville, Iowa says, 'His grandfather died when he (Joseph) was about seven or eight years old. He died at Zachariah Hole's in Darke County, Ohio.' At the date of this writing Joseph Hole was in his eighty-eighth year. He was probably nearer thirteen or fourteen years old at date of his grandfather's death, as a recently discovered record says that Daniel Hole died in 1814. Both these aged grandsons assert that their grandfather Hole came from England. Daniel had a large family and his line will now be traced as far as it has been possible to obtain names and dates.

DANIEL HOLE (Generation No 27, in William I line) was born in Nottinghamshire, England, in 1730, and was the youngest son of Jacob and Barbara Hole. He came, with his parents, to America, and in 1757 and 1758 we find him in Virginia. His wife's name was Phebe. He is said to have died in Ohio, either in Preble or Darke Co. (His grandson says "*in Darke Co.*") at the age of eighty-four years. Daniel and Phebe Hole had seven children:

(I.)   DANIEL HOLE, (Generation 28) born April 15, 1757, married Mary Beadell (daughter of William and Esther Beadell,) who was born July 7th, 1767; had issue nine children.

29TH GENERATION.   1st.   Phebe, born in New Jersey, Nov 4, 1785.
   2nd.   Esther, born in Virginia, July 12th, 1788.
   3rd.   Nancy, born in Kentucky, April 10th, 1790.
   4th.   Lydia, born in Cincinnati, Ohio, April 30th, 1793.
   5th.   Stephen, born in Cincinnati, Ohio, July 12th, 1795.
   6th.   Catherine, born at Beadell's Station, Oct. 7th, 1797.
   7th.   Aaron, born at Beadell's Station, Aug. 31, 1799.
   8th.   Mary, born at Beadell's Station, June 27th, 1803.
   9th.   Elizabeth, born at Beadell's Station, Jan. 25th, 1806.

Mary, wife of Daniel Hole, died April 12, 1829, aged 61 years. Daniel Hole died March 2nd, 1840, aged 83 years. This Daniel received a pension, from the time he was 76 years old, until his death, for services in the Revolutionary War. He enlisted in Hampshire Co., Virginia, and continued in service one year and five months, with Capt. James Hand and General Parsons. After moving successively (and *excessively*) through Virginia, New Jersey, Kentucky and

Ohio, he settled for some 25 years in Warren County, Ohio, at Beadell's Station, but in 1820 again moved and went with his children to Washington County, Indiana, where he died, as above stated, in 1840. Mary Beadell, wife of Daniel Hole, died April 12, 1829, aged 61 years.

Of their children, (Generation 30) we can give but a brief account.

29TH GENERATION.—(1st.) Phebe Hole, married 1st, a Clark and had one son, who also had one son, named Columbus Clark.

(2nd.) Esther Hole, married a Bowers and had a large family; sons named Nathan, Daniel, George, James and others.

(3rd.) Nancy Hole, married Nathaniel Moss, a minister, and left no family.

(4th.) Lydia, married Daniel Clark (brother to Phebe's husband), had three sons: William H., Daniel and Nathan. Nathan died unmarried, William H. had a son, George R. Clark, and a daughter, Lydia Clark.

(5th.) Stephen Hole, married Mary Eldy, at Lebanon, Ohio, in 1818, had issue,

30TH GENERATION.—(1st.) James Hervey, born Nov. 9, 1818, died Sept. 3, 1871. (See next page.)

(2nd.) Joseph Eddy, left issue, C. C. Hole and daughter, Mary E. who married Ephraim Everest, Marysville, Mo.

(3rd.) Daniel Perry, had Perry L, Harry S, and Sallie Reed.

(4th.) Phebe Ellen Hole never married.

(5th.) John Newton Hole, one daughter, Emma Lown.

(6th.) Mary Ann never married.

Stephen Hole married 2nd, Lucinda Mitchell, and had issue,

(7th.) Thomas Alexander Hole, now living in Havana, Illinois, and has 3 children, William and Grant Hole, and a daughter, Effie Sarf.

(8th.) William H. Hole, of Mason City, Illinois, has son, Dr. Burton Hole, Tallula, Illinois, and a daughter Mrs. Grant Chestnut.

(9th.) Sarah E. Hole, married James Covington, left issue two sons, Stephen and William Covington.

(10th.) Louisa M. married Robert Lofton, had issue Frank, Charles, Eli and Fred Lofton.

(11th.) Robert M. Hole died unmarried.

(12th.) Nancy C. Hole, married Captain Samuel Whitaker, no issue.

30TH GENERATION.—(1st.) JAMES H. HOLE, 1818-1871, married Mary E. Wible, had issue,

31ST GENERATION.—]1.] Henry F. Hole, born 1842, married Susan D. Cadwalder, Jan. 21st, 1864. She died Jan. 21st, 1890. Had issue,

32ND. GENERATION.—Elmer C. of 6424 Peoria Street, Chicago, Ill.

(2nd.) Charles B. of Effingham, Kansas.

(3rd.) Franklin J., Mt. Clemens, Mich.

(4th.) Myra C. Hole of the Yerks Observatory, Williams Bay, Wis.

(5th.) John H. Hole, Rolfe, Iowa.

(6th.) Katherine Hole, Fairbury, Nebraska.

Henry F. Hole married 2nd. Elizabeth McGibbon who has issue,

(7th.) Frances Lillian Hole, born July 30, 1900.

29TH. GENERATION.— 6th. Catherine Hole (1797), married Thomas Brittain and had issue, William, Ellen, Mary, Alla, Stephen, Sarah, Elizabeth and Susan Brittain.

(7th.) Aaron Hole, 1799, married a Brittain, had issue, James B. Hole of Illinois.

(8th.) Mary Hole, 1803, married a Smith, had one son, Daniel Hole Smith, who married Elizabeth Hinds and had issue several children.

(9th.) Elizabeth Hole, 1806, married Robert Mitchell, had issue (1) Thomas, married Martha A. Colglazier.

(2nd.) Daniel, killed by lightning.

(3rd.) Ellen, married David Colglazier.

(4th.) Kate, married Daniel Kern.

(5th.) Stephen H. married Maria Purkhiser.

(6th.) Robert H. married Eliza J. Carr.

31ST. GENERATION.—(2nd) Hannah Minerva Hole, 1845, married Thomas Jones, has issue (1) Frank Lyman Jones.

(2nd.) S. Minot Jones, an attorney, Chicago, Ill.

(3rd.) Pollie A. Hole, 1847, married Rev. Thomas J. Keith, a missionary to India, now living in Chicago. Had issue one son, Henry Boyd who died when 21 years of age.

(4.) Harriet Reed Hole, married Captain Samuel Whitaker, and had issue John (deceased), Nellie and Daisy of Vincennes, Indiana. Harriet Reed Whitaker is deceased.

(5.) Clara Urble Hole married Arthur E. Hunt. She died, leaving one daughter, Alice Hunt, now of Shenandoah, Iowa.

(6.) James Samuel Hole, married Celia Hill, no issue. They live at Harbine, Jefferson County, Neb.

(7.) Stephen Lincoln Hole, born 1860, married Anna Murphy; issue Andrew, Lester and Vernon Hole, of Effingham, Kansas.

30TH GENERATION.—(2.) Daniel P. Hole, 1823-1887, married Ona S. Taylor, had issue (1), Sallie Hole, married Michael Reed of Hastings, Neb.; issue 1 son and 1 daughter. (2) Henry Stephen Hole, unmarried, Hastings, Neb. (3) Perry L. Hole, married, lives in Chicago. Has two sons, Dean Hole and McPherson Hole.

(3.) John N. Hole, 1830-1888, married Jennie Lester; has issue. Emma Hole, married Frank Town. They have three daughters and all reside in Ogden, Utah.

28TH GENERATION.—[2.] William Hole, born 1759, 28th of April, married Ruth Crane in New Jersey; moved to Ohio, via Kentucky. They had eleven children, six boys and five girls: Charles, Jonathan, William, Joseph, Daniel, Jay, Sarah, Anna, Ruth, Phebe and Mary. A letter written by Joseph is given on a preceding page.

[3.] Zachariah Hole lived at Hole's Station, now Miamisburgh; moved to Preble County, Ohio, and then to Montgomery County, where he died. Had a family of three boys and six girls.

[4.] Dr. John Hole, the first known physician in our family in America, lived on Hole Creek, Montgomery County, where he died. He married Hannah Clark and for a time resided in New Jersey. The writer during a recent visit to the old burying ground at Madison, New Jersey, was attracted by two extremely ancient looking flat tombstones, and upon scraping the snow from the inscriptions was surprised to find that one was the tombstone of William Hole, an infant son of the above named Dr. John Hole and Hannah Clark. The two interesting inscriptions read as follows:

"Here lies ye body of

MR. AARON BURNET,

who died in September, A. D., 1755, in ye 100th year of his age"

And

"In memory of

WILLIAM,

son of John and Hannah Hole, who departed this life October the 11th, 1797, in the 7th year of his age."

—63—

This Aaron Burnet was probably the grandfather of William Burnet, member of the Continental Congress, and great-grandfather of Hon. Jacob Burnet, U. S. Senator from Ohio. While the little child beside him was a great-grandson of the emigrant Jacob Hole, of Caunton, England.

(5th.) Elizabeth Hole, married John Craig and is said to have raised eleven children. [Not traced in this book.]

[6th.] Mary Hole, married a Yazel, and had six children; three boys and three girls.

[7th.] Phebe Hole, married Anthony Badgley, in New Jersey.

This completes the genealogy of three sons of the founder of the Hole family in America, viz: Peter [1717-1825]; John [1721-1784], and Daniel, [1730-1814.] There remains yet the third son, Charles Hole, who left an immense posterity. In the next chapter the line of Charles Hole will be traced.

CHAPTER XI.

xcepting the descendants of their oldest son, Jacob, whose line will be
traced in the next chapter.)

27TH GENERATION.—Charles Hole was born in Nottinghamshire,
England, in August [?] 1728. Came to Bucks County, Pa., in
1740; married Mary, daughter of John McGinnis, in 1757. (Mary
McGinnis had a half-sister, Ellen Haig, who lived in Wayne
County, Indiana.) Charles was raised by a family of Friends (or
Quakers,) named Edwards, but he was not a member of the
Society of Friends. In 1858, after the birth of their first child,
Charles and Mary Hole removed to Loudoun County, Virginia,
and in 1792 again removed to Bedford County, Virginia, where
he died, near or in Lynchburgh, in December 1803, in the 76th
year of his age. Mary Hole, his widow, came to Columbiana
County, Ohio, in 1805 and died at Carmel in July, 1815, aged 77
years. Charles and Mary Hole had issue eleven children:

28TH GENERATION.—[1.] Jacob Hole, born February 27th, 1758,
died February 1st, 1842.

[2.] Nathan Hole, born 1759, died 1828.

[3.] Levi Hole, born 1761, died 1803.

[4.] Rebecca Hole, born 1763, died 1825.

[5.] Mary Hole, born March 7th, 1768, died March 11th, 1849.

[6.] David Hole, born Aug. 19th, 1770, died Feb. 10th, 1854.

[7.] Jonah Hole, born 1772, was living in 1828.

[8.] John Hole, born 1774, died in childhood.

[9.] Ann Hole, born November 5th, 1777, died Oct., 1855.

[10.] Tacy Hole, born 1779, died 1828.

[11.] Elizabeth Hole, born 1780, died December 23d, 1865.

Leaving the family of the oldest son, Jacob, for another chapter,
we will trace the families of the other ten children of Charles and
Mary Hole.

28TH GENERATION.—[2.] Nathan Hole, second son of Charles and
Mary Hole, went with his parents to Bedford County, Va., in

1792 where he joined the Society of Friends. He came to Ohio in 1805 and became a minister in the Friends Church. He never married, and died in 1828.

The will of the Rev. Nathan Hole is here given in part. "I, Nathan Hole, of Middleton Township, Columbiana County, Ohio, farmer, being weak in body but of sound mind and memory [through divine favor] do make and publish this my last will and testament in form following to wit. *   *   *   *   *   *

I give and bequeath to my brother David Hole or his legal heirs all the land included within the following described bounds * * * * provided my said brother David shall pay, within a reasonable time, the sum of ten dollars to my brother Jonah Hole, and five dollars to Miriam Hole, the widow of my brother Levi Hole, or their legal heirs. I give and bequeath to my sisters, Ann, Tacy and Elizabeth, or their legal heirs, the remaining part of said quarter-section and bounded as follows: *   *   *   *   I will to my sister Elizabeth one horse; the one she may choose. It is my will and desire that all my stock, farming utensils, household and kitchen furniture be sold and the proceeds of the same, together with all money collected from debts due and owing to my estate, be equally divided among my brother Jacob, sister Mary and brother-in-law John M. Edgar, or their legal heirs. I will to my brother Jonah, or his legal heirs, ten dollars and to my sister-in-law Miriam Hole or her legal heirs, five dollars; the said sums of ten and five dollars to be paid by my brother David Hole as hereinbefore provided. I will and bequeath all my wearing apparel to my nephew Nathan Hole, (*son of Jacob and Mary Hole.*) I ordain and appoint my nephews, Charles Hole and Joseph Heald executors of this my last will and testament. In testimony whereof I have hereunto set my hand and seal this 24th day of the third month, in the year of our Lord one thousand eight hundred and twenty eight."

"NATHAN HOLE"

[3.] Levi Hole, born 1761. Did not remove to Bedford County but died in Loudoun County, Va., and was buried at Goose Creek burying ground, (now *Lincoln.*) His death occurred when he was little past forty years old and he left a widow, Miriam Hole, and two daughters. No trace whatever has been found of the daughters. The line is probably extinct. The writer has a letter written by Miriam Hole, in 1845 when she was eighty years of age. Nathan [2] and Levi [3] appear not to have owned land in Loudoun County, Virginia. The writer has a bond or note signed by these brothers, which reads as follows:

"We, the subscribers do promise and oblige ourselves and our heirs to pay or cause to be paid unto George W. Fairfax, Esq., or to his heirs, the full and just sum of 2 pounds, 4 shillings, 8 pence, with lawful interest from date hereof, on or before the 4th day of February, 1786, to satisfy the said George W. Fairfax, Esq., for rents due him to this date, as witness our hands and seal this 4th day of November, 1785."   "NATHAN HOLE,"
                                            "LEVI HOLE."

"Sealed and delivered in the presence of John Bagley."

[4th.] Rebecca Hole, born 1763, married John M. Edgar and removed to Ohio in 1804. She died at Carmel, Columbiana Co., Ohio, in 1825. Rebecca and John Edgar had four children, three of whom died in childhood. The fourth, Ellen Edgar, died in Mt. Union, Stark Co., Ohio, and was buried at Carmel. John M. Edgar died in Mt. Union, [now Alliance], Ohio, in 1860, in the 100th year of his age. The grave of this Centenarian, which was a few years ago identified by Mrs. Maria Antram, who well knew the Edgars and who still lives near Alliance, is now entirely obliterated, and the tombstone is lost. Rebecca and John M. Edgar have no living posterity.

[5th.] Mary Hole, born March 7th, 1768, joined Friends in Bedford County, Va., was married to Jason Morlan and removed to Ohio in 1801 or 1802. Jason Morlan was born in Virginia, July 9, 1772 and died in Washington County, Ohio, Nov. 25, 1849. Mary Morlan died in Washington County, Ohio, March 11th, 1849, aged nearly 81 years. Jason and Mary Morlan had issue five children, four of whom lived to maturity.

29TH GENERATION.—[Charles Morlan, born Feb. 26, 1803, died Dec. 31, 1852.

[2nd.] Ann Morlan, born Jan. 10, 1805, died Nov. 17, 1885.

[3rd.] Martha Morlan, born Nov. 1, 1807, died Nov. 28, 1874.

[4th.] William Hole Morlan, born Oct. 25, 1816, died Mar. 4, 1855.

Of the above named children of Jason and Mary Morlan, [1] Charles died in Washington County without issue.

(2nd.) Ann Morlan, married John Marshall, May 25th, 1842 and died Nov. 17, 1885, aged nearly 81 years, leaving one daughter.

30TH. GENERATION.—Martha E. Marshall, born March 5th, 1843, married Benjamin J. Hobson, Sept. 24, 1862, died Feb. 1st, 1881 having had issue,

31ST. GENERATION.—(1st.) Emma Hobson, Sept. 7, 1864, died Aug. 14, 1868,

(2nd.) Thomas A. born Nov. 12, 1868.

(3rd.) Arthur B. born Mar. 16, 1871.

(4th.) William C. born Nov. 10, 1874, married Laura Gorham Mar. 26, 1898.

29TH. GENERATION.—(3rd.) Martha Morlan, born Nov. 1, 1807, married William Addis, Oct. 7, 1832, died Nov. 28, 1874, had issue seven children.

30TH. GENERATION. —Mary Addis, born Aug. 23, 1833, married a Thurston, lives in Indiana.

(2nd.) Creighton Addis, born Aug. 17, 1835, died June 15, 1886.

(3rd.) Benj. F. Addis, born Sept. 4, 1838, died May 24, 1879.

(4th.) Jason Addis, born July 21, 1842, deceased.

(5th.) John R. Addis, born Nov. 2 1844, Cutler, O.

(6th.) Marshall Addis, born Oct. 8, 1847, died Feb. 6, 1867.

(7th.) Charles M. Addis, born July 3, 1850, Cutler, O. Has one daughter, aged 16, name not given.

[4.] William Hole Morlan, born Oct. 25, 1816, married April 12, 1838, Winifred Pickering and died March 4, 1855, had issue,

XXX.—[1.] Ann C. Morlan, born May 17, 1839, died Oct. 3, 1854.

[2.] Sarah J. Morlan, born Aug. 2, 1841, died Jan. 14, 1897.

[3.] Jason E. Morlan, born Aug. 8, 1844, died Jan. 5, 1876.

[4.] Martha S. Morlan, born April 14, 1849, died Feb. 9, 1865.

[5.] Mary E. Morlan, born July 10, 1852.

Sarah J. Morlan, [2] married Samuel G. Kille, April 18, 1858 and had issue 6 children,

XXXI—[1.] Mary Etta Kille, born March, 28, 1862, married William Kemble, May 23, 1894, Salem, Ohio, and has children, Bernice and Lois.

[2.] Ellsworth Kille, born Oct. 2, 1864, married Retta Vogal, Oct 17, 1879 and has Grace, Charles, Etta, Lincoln and Lester.

[3.] Myrtle L. Kille, born Nov. 3, 1871 married K. L. Coburn and has son Frank.

(4,) William L. Kille, born Jan. 31, 1874, deceased.

(5.) Mabel I. Kille, born June 12, 1878.

(6.) Elizabeth Kille, born July 25, 1883.

30th GENERATION.—[3.] Jason E. Morlan, married Martha E. Naylor, 1867 and had issue,

31st GENERATION.—[1.] Allison E., born July 1, 1868, married Tenie Whitlatch, in 1888, died Apr., 1903; had issue 6 children: Mattie C., Fred L., Sarah E., Rachel E., Goldie L. and Clyde.

[2.] Winifred C. Morlan, born March 24, 1872, died March 5, 1896.

[3.] John A. Morlan, born June 28, 1874, deceased.

30th GENERATION.—[5.] Mary E. Morlan, married Asa D. Hallett, July 10, 1870, in Marietta, Ohio, and had issue,

31st GENERATION.—[1.] Alda Clyde Hallett, born May 31, 1871, died Nov. 25, 1902.

[2.] Norma Maude, born Jan. 25, 1873, died April 5, 1873.

[3.] Zenas Claude, born Aug. 31, 1874, married Dec. 1, 1903 to Catherine Schultheis, of Warner, O.

(4th.) Winnefred Morlan, born Dec. 31st, 1878.

[5th.] Anna Lulu, born May 4, 1881, married Jan. 23, 1902 Clarence E. Powell and had son Hallett Powell, born Aug. 24, 1903.

[6th.] Baby May Hallett, born June 27, 1884, died July 6, 1884.

[7th.] Augustus Carl, born May 6, 1886.

[8th.] Corwin, born Apr. 8, 1888, died Sept. 20, 1838.

[9th.] Chester Ray, born Oct. 3, 1890, and died Jan. 1, 1891.

[10th.] Mary Golden, born Mar. 16th, 1893.

28TH. GENERATION.—DAVID HOLE, born Aug. 19, 1770, died Feb. 10, 1854. Came to Ohio from Bedford County, Virginia in 1804. He married Anna Howell, who was born Oct. 17th, 1779 and died Sept. 2nd, 1844. David and Anna Hole had a family of nine children.

29TH. GENERATION.—[1.] Elon Hole, born Nov. 22, 1800, died Jan. 27, 1895, in his 95th year, married Beulah Ann Pettit, and had six children [Gen. 30] Catherine, Charles, Beulah Ann, Lydia, David and Anna.

[2nd.] Catherine Hole, born Dec. 25, 1802, died June 10, 1825, married Robert Miller and died without issue, [See Miller Family]

[3rd.] Tacey Hole, born Feb. 21, 1805, died Aug. 13th, 1848, married Caleb Hawley and died without issue.

[4th.] Jesse Hole, born Aug. 15th, 1808, lives in Marshalltown Iowa, marr e l Susannah Heacock, Dec. 20th, 1837, and has issue, seven children.

30TH. GENERATION.--[1.] Oliver Rush Hole, born Feb. 22, 1840, died Nov. 4, 1840.

(2nd.) Hannah Louese Hole, born Nov. 30th, 1842, lives with her father, Jesse Hole, in Marshalltown, Iowa.

(3rd.l Osborn Howell Hole, born Oct. 19th, 1844, married Maria E. Ellis, Feb, 18, 1884. No issue.

[4th,] Jonathan Lloyd Hole, born May 17th, 1847, married Malinda S. Cope, Feb. 16th, 1870, died Sept. 17th, 1901. Had issue three children, Nettie Hole who died unmarried; Adalie L. married William Lineaweaver, and have one child, William Lineaweaver; Harry E. Hole, who married Fern Foreman. No children.

[5.] David Earnest Hole, born March 2nd, 1849, married Mary Raley, August 14, 1886, has issue, two children; Esther and Jessie Hole.

[6.] Sarah Adeline Hole, born April 8th, 1853, married William Saling; died June 25th, 1889. No issue.

[7.] Mary Leona, born June 25th, 1855, married Frank E. Whealen. Died January 26th, 1885, without issue.

29TH GENERATION—[5.] Terzah Hole, born December 4th, 1810, married Evan Lodge, died aged 78 years in 1888; had issue, 8 children [Gen. 30] viz: Abel, David, Jonathan, Herod, Elizabeth, Emily, Alice and Jane.

[6,] Mary Hole, born March 28th. 1813, married Solomon Teegarden and died without issue in 1896, aged 83 years.

[7.] Narcissa Hole, born May 11th, 1816, married Jonathan Humphrey; died, aged 77 years and left issue, six children [Gen. 30] viz: Seth, Joseph, John, Evan, Mary and Anna.

[8.] Ruth Hole, born October 30, 1818, married Joshua Barton; died in 1899, aged 81 years, leaving issue [Gen. 30], John, Mary Catherine and Frances Barton.

[9.] Anna Hole, born October 20th, 1821, died August 19th, 1823. Of the nine children of David and Anna Hole, six have lived to a great age, viz: Narcissa, 77; Terzah, 78; Ruth. 81; Mary, 83; Elon, 95; and Jesse is still living and in his 95th year. This, at the present time shows an average of 85 years, a record probably unequaled.

From "The Friend's Review."

HOLE—Died, at the residence of his daughter, in Des Moines, Iowa, First month 27th, 1895, Elon Hole, in the ninety-fifth year of his age. He had been a faithful member of the Society of Friends all of his life. Born in Bedford county, Va., he removed with his family to Ohio at an early age, and thence went at manhood to Pennsylvania, from when ce he removed back to Ohio, and later to the then new country and almost wilderness of Indiana. The very long and useful life came to a close peacefully both in body and mind. The immediate cause of his death was a fall sustained four days before, which, superinduced by his extreme old age, terminated the life of one who had ever been faithful in the Master's kingdom, and who had always "done with his might what his hand found to do."

The descendants of Elon Hole were not given under the heading Generation 29, [1.] and will be given here.

30TH GENERATION—[1.] Beulah Ann Hole, married Talbot Ware and had issue.

31ST GENERATION.—Wilmer C. Ware, Anna Ware, Ella Ware, Alfred Ware, Howard Ware and Edith Ware.

30TH GENERATION.—(2.) Lydia Hole, married Nathan Armstrong, had issue.

31ST GENERATION.—Harry, Walter and Frank Armstrong.

30TH GENERATION.—(3.) Anna Hole, married Martin Bugre, had issue.

31ST GENERATION.—Four children, Ezra, Emerson, Foster and a fourth deceased.

30TH GENERATION.—(4.) Catharine, married Elijah Farr and had issue.

31TH GENERATION.—Frank, Annie, Elizabeth, Hartwell, Levi Morton, Lula Belle, Dolph and one deceased.

30TH GENERATION.—(5 and 6.) Charles and David Hole left no descendants.

28TH GENERATION.—(7.) JONAH HOLE, born 1772, never left Virginia, date of death not known. He was living in 1828 when his brother Nathan wrote his will. Jonah married Betsy Howell, who died at the birth of her only child, Ury B. Hole. He afterwards married Nancy Wilson, in Bedford Co., Va., and had a family. No trace whatever of this second edition of Jonah Hole's family can be obtained.

29TH GENERATION.—[1.] Ury B. Hole, daughter of Jonah and Betsy Hole, was born in Bedford county, Virgina, June 26th, 1796. Married Joseph Heald, born Feb. 14, 1791, died 1860 leaving issue thirteen children:

30TH GENERATION.—(1.) Hiel Heald, born Nov. 1st, 1817, died Oct. 29th, 1864.

(2.) Penina Heald, born Mar. 1st, 1819, married Samuel Shaw deceased.

(3.) Phebe Elma Heald, born July 18th, 1820, married Silas Allman.

(4.) Betsy H. Heald, born May 12th, 1823, married Edwin Hollingsworth.

(5.) Elmira Heald, born Aug. 5th, 1825, married Caleb Marshall Sept. 25th, 1847.

(6.) Ann Heald, born Jan. 14th, 1828, deceased.

(7.) Nathan H. Heald, (twin) born Jan. 14th, 1828, married Mary S. Kees, deceased.

[8.] Jonah Heald, born Feb. 29th, 1830, deceased.

[9.] Mary Ruanna Heald, born Jan. 28th, 1832, deceased.

[10.] John Heald, born Aug. 24th, 1833, deceased.

(11.) Anna M., born April 23, 1836, married Samuel N. Hobson.

(12.) Abner J., born December 5th, 1836, married Martha Brown, and 2nd, Florence Kingsbury.

(13.) Martha Jane, born April 17th, 1839, married David Bruce, deceased.

CHILDREN OF PENINA HEALD SHAW.

31ST GENERATION.—(2.) 1. Hiel Shaw, born August 3d, 1839, deceased.

(2.) 2. Seth Shaw, born April 17, 1843, married Martha Ashton.

CHILDREN OF PHEBE HEALD ALLMAN.

[31.] 1. Lucy Ann Allman, born September 5th, 1841, married Harvey Ward, deceased.

(3.) 2. Levi Allman, born April 18th, 1843, married Mary Landon, deceased.

(3.) 3. Jas. B. Allman, born Jan. 15, 1846, married Jennie Courtney.

[3.] 4. Mary Reanna Allman, born January 31st, 1853, married Charles A. McCrea.

BETSY HOLLINGSWORTH'S CHILDREN.

[4.] 1. Ury B. Hollingsworth, born September 29th, 1846, married David Ellis.

[4.] 2. Sarah Hollingsworth, born February 19th, 1852, married Charles Blackburn.

[4.] 3. Penina Hollingsworth, born September 13th, 1854, married Francis Dean.

[4.] 4. Mary A. Hollingsworth, born April 15th, 1865, married Nathan Thomason.

ELMIRA MARSHALL'S CHILDREN.

[5.] 1. Anna Maria Marshall. * [See great-grandchildren.]

[5.] 2. Ury Etta Marshall. * [See great-grandchildren.]

NATHAN H. HEALD'S CHILDREN.

[7.] 1. Sarah Ruanna Heald, born September 18, 1851, deceased.

[7.] 2. John K. Heald, born August 10th, 1852, deceased.

[7.] 3. William A. Heald, born Aug. 24th, 1854, deceased.

[7.] 4. Elma Alice Heald, born Feb. 29th, 1856.

[7.] 5. Abner T. Heald, born Aug. 10th, 1857.

[7.] 6. Martha E. Heald, born May 26th, 1859.

[7.] 7. Joseph E. Heald, born Apr. 21 1861, deceased.

[7.] 8. Hiel Heald, born June 26th, 1864.

JOHN HEALD'S CHILDREN.

31st GENERATION. [10.]—1. Thomas J. Heald, born Nov. 1, 1868.

2. Alvin Heald, born Sept. 6, 1870, deceased.

3. Elizabeth S. Heald, born March 25, 1872, deceased.

ANNE M. HOBSON'S CHILDREN.

31st GENERATION. [11.]—1. Marianna, born Aug. 22, 1855, married J. A. Lovell.

2. Adeliza, born Apr. 22, 1857, married O. M. Lovell.

3. Rebekah Estella, born Mar. 6, 1876, married E. R. Lash, Jr.

ABNER J. HEALD'S CHILDREN.

31ST. GENERATION [12] 1.—John B. Heald, born Dec. 25th, 1869.

MARTHA JANE BRUCE'S CHILDREN.

31ST GENERATION [13] 1.—Florence Nightingale, born Aug. 16, 1862, deceased.

2. Lenora G, born Dec. 23, 1863.
3. Loretta Florence, born Nov. 12, 1865.
4. J. Howard, born Nov. 6, 1867.
5. Addie Adell, born June 1, 1870.
6. Birdie E, born Sept. 3, 1873, deceased.

GREAT-GRAND-CHILDREN OF URY B. HEALD.

GRAND-CHILDREN OF PHEBE ALLMAN. 30. (3.)

32ND GENERATION.—Harold Lester, son of Levi Allman, born Jan. 29, 1871.

Austin Lester, son of James Allman and Mary McCrea, deceased.

GRAND CHILDREN OF BETSY HOLLINGSWORTH. 30. (8.)

32ND GENERATION.—Ludana W., daughter of Ury Ellis, (31), (4) 1), born Sept. 8, 1865.

Elizabeth, daughter of Ury Ellis, (31, (4), 1), born Nov. 28, 1873, deceased.

Edwin D., son of Ury Ellis, born May 9, 1876.

Louisa B., daughter of Ury Ellis, born March 24, 1880, deceased.

Hervey G., son of Ury Ellis, born June 17, 1882.

Eliza W. Blackburn, daughter of Sarah Blackburn, (31, (4) 2), born Apr. 20, 1876.

Anna P., daughter of Sarah Blackburn, born Dec. 13, 1878.

Jessie H., daughter of Sarah Blackburn, born May 9, 1880.

Mary Elma, daughter of Sarah Blackburn, born Nov. 9, 1886.

Rolland, son of Sarah Blackburn, born Dec. 19, 1895.

Williard, son of Sarah Blackburn, born Feb. 23, 1898.

Almeda B. Dean, daughter of Penina Dean, (31, (4), 3), born Nov. 19, 1875, deceased.

Caroline, daughter of Penina Dean, born June 11, 1879.

Ida J., daughter of Penina Dean, born Nov. 20, 1883.

Rolinda, daughter of Penina Dean, born Nov., 1895,

Arthur Everett Thomason, son of Mary A., (31, (4),4), Sept. 21, 1888.

Earl Thomason, son of Mary A., born Oct. 5, 1889.

Alice Eunice Thomason, daughter of Mary A., ⎰ twins, born
Edna B. Thomason, daughter of Mary A., ⎱ April 20, 1892.

Edith Thomason, daughter of Mary A., born Dec. 7, 1895.

Foster Thomason, son of Mary A., born Feb. 1, 1898.

Irene Thomason, daughter, of Mary A., born Feb. 25, 1901, deceased.

Ernest N. Thomason, son of Mary A., born April 30, 1902.

GRANDCHILDREN OF ANNE M. HOBSON, 30 (11)

32ND GENERATION.—Jesse M. Lovell, daughter of Marianna Lovell, (31(11)1) born June 8, 1873.

Annie J. Lovell, daughter of Marianna Lovell, born Nov. 19, 1877.

Paul V. Lovell, ⎰ twins, sons of Marianna Lovell, born Oct. 24,
Earl B. Lovell, ⎱ 1879.

Alice W. Lovell, daughter of Marianna Lovell, born Nov. 6, 1885.

Helen Fostine Lovell, daughter of Marianna Lovell, born Feb. 7, 1890.

Lucile Lovell (daughter of Adeliza Lovell), Aug. 3, 1880.

GRANDCHILDREN OF ELMIRA MARSHALL, 30 (5).

31ST GENERATION.—(1.) Anna Maria Marshall married John Morton Kiehl; had issue, Effie Glendora, Florence Elma and Roy C. Kiehl. Effie Glendora Kiehl married Geo. W. Hollester and has issue,

XXXIII.—Zeta Maria, Kenneth and Glen Hollister.

XXXI.—(2). Ury Etta Marshall, daughter of Elmira Marshall, born June 28, 1855, married John T. Baughman and had issue,

XXXII.—(1.) Austin M., born in Cass County, Iowa, Dec. 14, 1878, married Etta V. Burough, July 23, 1902, and has Ruth Baughman, born July 26, 1903. A great-great grandchild of Ury B. Heald.

XXXII.—(2.) Cora E. Baughman, born July 2, 1880, Cass County, Iowa.

[3.] Raymond W. Baughman, born June 19, 1883, Cass Co., Ia.

[4.] Mabel J. Baughman, born May 2, 1886, Chase Co., Neb.

[5.] Clarence S. Baughman, born June 20, 1888, Chase Co., Neb.

[6.] Leslie C. Baughman, born Aug. 14, 1889, Chase Co., Neb.

[7.] Ethel M. Baughman, born Feb. 27, 1895, Chase Co., Neb.

[8.] Elwood D., Baughman, born Oct. 19, 1896, Cass Co., Ia.

GRANDCHILDREN OF MARTHA J. BRUCE, (30(13.)

31. [2] Lenora G. Bruce married Alton J. Milton and has sons. [1] Ward Milton, Feb. 10, 1891; [2] Bert Milton, June 2, 1892.

[3.] Loretta Bruce married M. U. B. Scribuer, Sept., 1901.

[4.] J. Howard Bruce married Aileen Conklin, Aug. 26, 1891, and has, [1] Ethel Loretta, Aug. 13, 1892; Edith Adell, June 2, 1894 [died July 22, 1894,] and [3] Dale Howard, Sept. 22, 1900.

Mrs. Annie Hobson, eleventh child of Ury B. Hole and Joseph Heald, is descended from Quaker parents, who were active Abolitionists as well. It would seem only natural that reform movements in every department of life should be regarded as paramount questions by the subject of this sketch. The Temperance question early enlisted the sympathy of Mrs. Hobson who was a member of the Good Templars in its most active period just after the close of the civil war. She served as Worthy Chief Templar one year and Delegate to State Convention while a citizen of Beverly, O., in 1865.

The Woman's Relief Corps was organized soon after, its purpose being the relief of families of veterans of the Civil War. Mrs. Hobson with the wives, mothers and daughters of soldiers, united as Charter Members of Columbus Golden Corps, No. 32, in Athens, O., where she has served as President, Secretary, Assistant Inspector, State and National Delegate, and is still a member.

Mrs. Hobson was a member of the Chautauqua Circle of Athens until the organization of the Pallas Club in 1893, and has been honored with official positions in this organization, also being Delegate to the State Federation.

While all these organizations have tended to enlighten and broaden the understanding, the enfranchisement of women appeals the strongest to Mrs. Hobson as being the direct and only plausible way to achieve the objects sought in all the others, and also because an enlightened and responsible motherhood only, can produce the highest type of manhood.

Mrs. Hobson is at present the presiding officer of the local Suffrage Club and has served as State Treasurer Auditor and State and National Delegate.

Though at an age when most women are content and even anxious to give up the active labors of life, she is now most enthusiastic. During the summer of 1903 she was one of the first to agitate a Village Improvement Association, which has shaped her home town into one of the prettiest and cleanest in the country.

29TH GENERATION.—[8.] John Hole, born 1774, died in boyhood.

[9.] Ann Hole, born Nov. 5th, 1777, married Levi Miller, June 28th, 1819, [See Miller family] and raised a large family of step-children. Had no children of her own. Was for many years and Elder, in Sandy Spring Monthly Meeting, survived her husband and died in Oct.,1855 at the home of her sister Elizabeth Cooper, at Sandy Spring.

[10.] Tacy Hole, born 1779, married Daniel Mercer. Had but one child, Ruth, who married John Wise. Ruth had one daughter, Lucretia, who died at 5 years of age. Tacy Hole Mercer was an Elder in Middleton Monthly Meeting. She died in 1828. Daniel Mercer married again and died in Iowa about 1866 at between 90 and 100 years of age.

[11.] Elizabeth Hole, born 1780, married Calvin Cooper [born May, 1772, son of George and Susanna Cooper of Lancaster county, Pa. Died, aged eighty-eight years.] Had no family but raised a family of eight step-children. She died at Sandy Spring, Columbiana county, Ohio, Dec. 23d, 1865, aged eighty six years.

CHAPTER XII.

THE DESCENDANTS OF JACOB HOLE AND MARY (THOMAS) HOLE.

GENERATION XXVIII.

(Excepting the decendants of their two oldest sons, Charles and John Hole.)

Jacob, (XXVIII) son of Charles and Mary Hole (XXVII) was born in Bucks County, Penn., Feb. 27, 1758, was taken by his parents to Loudoun County, Virginia, when he was about three months old. Loudoun County had been erected the previous year, from Fairfax, and was named in honor of the Earl of Loudoun, who was commander of the military affairs in America during the latter part of the French and Indian War. As Loudoun County has been the home of so many of the Holes, anything pertaining to the history of that county should be of value to the family. Jacob Hole married in 1782, Mary Thomas, daughter of Captain John Thomas, (XXVII) of Leesburg, and settled in the northern part of the county amongst the German emigrants. Howe's History informs us that "there is a very considerable contrast observable in the different sections of this county." "That part lying northwest of Waterford was origin-ally settled by *Germans*, and is called the *German Settlement*. The middle of the county southwest of Waterford and west of Leesburg, was mostly settled by emigrants from the Middle States, many of whom were Friends."   *   *   *   *   *   "The Quakers in Virginia suffered much persecution at an early day. In the Revo-lution, their non-conformity to the military law of the State, from conscientious motives, brought them into difficulty." Here then it is probable that Jacob Hole, living amongst the German people, ac-quired enough of their language to be able to speak it imperfectly, and his narration of some of the history of his neighbors and friends became confused with that of his own family. Mary Thomas, his, wife, was a descendant of some of the best English families. Her father was born in London, and was an officer in the French and Indian and Revolutionary War. It seems highly improbable that the Holes were of German origin or that any of them ever spoke the German language until she and her husband settled in the German end of Loudoun County. In 1787 they removed and settled near Goose Creek Meeting, now called Lincoln, and in 1793 again removed and settled in Bedford County, Virginia. Here they remained for a period of 22 years. Seven children were born to them while living in Loudoun County and four more after removing to Bedford County. In 1815 Jacob and Mary Hole came to Columbiana County, Ohio, and settled on the farm now owned by Nathan Pim, about 2 miles from East Rochester and near the Augusta Friends' Meeting House.

In 1816, or within a year after his arrival in Ohio, Jacob Hole, assisted by his sons, built the log "Meeting House," near his home, then and ever since known as "Augusta Friends' Meeting House." He and his wife joined the Society of Friends about this time, being near 60 years of age. They were useful and intelligent citizens and honored members of the Friends church until death. A very pleasing recollection of Jacob Hole was given to the writer by an aged friend of his great grand-parent, who well remembers seeing the aforesaid sporty ancestor riding to the hounds and galloping through Rochester, Ohio, his long gray hair flying in the breeze—having lost his hat, madly pursuing the fox, and all this when he was past eighty years of age.

Beat this, very Reverend Dean Hole (of Rochester, England,) if you can! To Jacob and Mary Hole were born eleven children, six sons and five daughters, all of whom lived to maturity, only one child died before the death of the father, (Hannah Perdue, in 1841, at the age of 55) and the eleven sons and daughters, with the father and mother, died at an average age of almost 75 years. A most remarkable average for a family of thirteen persons. Jacob Hole lived to see the 78 grand-children and Mary his widow survived to see the 81st grandchild. Jacob died Feb. 1st, 1842, aged 84 years. Mary died in 1849, aged 92 years. Both were buried in the Friends' burying ground of Augusta Friend's Meeting, within half a mile of the home which they "took up" in 1816 and where they continued to reside until their death.

CHILDREN OF JACOB AND MARY [THOMAS] HOLE.

29TH GENERATION.—1. Charles Hole, born June 27th, 1783, died June 23d, 1854.

    2. John Hole, born Jan. 7th, 1785, died Feb. 3d, 1868.

    3. Hannah Hole Perdue, born Mar. 3d, 1786, died May 1841.

    4. Abi Hole Preston, born May 16th, 1788, died Mar. 23d, 1855.

    5. Rebecca Hole, born Oct. 3d, 1789, died Jan., 1843, unmarried.

    6. Sophia Hole, born Mar. 18th, 1791, died Feb. 4th, 1875, unmarried.

    7. Mahlon Hole, born Dec. 1st, 1792, died March, 1871.

8. Nathan Hole, born Apr. 3d, 1794, died Nov., 1862.

10. Mary Hole Green, born Mar. 20th, 1798, died Feb. 12th, 1883.

11. Jacob Hole, born Mar. 11th, 1802, died March 14th, 1873.

The descendants of Charles (1.) and John (2.) will be given in the next chapter. Rebecca Hole (5.) and Sophia Hole (6.) died unmarried. Rebecca was an extremely talented member of the family, being a writer of poetry and essays of no mean ability. Sophia, who lived to the age of eighty-four, was scholarly and possessed of an uncommonly good mind.

29TH GENERATION.—(3.) Hannah Hole, married in Virginia, Bennett Perdue, had issue eight children and died in Columbiana Co., Ohio in 1841, aged fifty-five. As none of her descendants have been willing to answer letters or give the least information in regard to family chronology it will only be possible to give here the names of Hannah Perdue's children.

30TH GENERATION.—(1.) Oliver P. Perdue.

(2.) William M. Perdue.

(3.) John S. Perdue.

(4.) Jacob Perdue.

(5.) Rezin J. Perdue.

(6.) Benjamin F. Perdue.

(7.) Franklin Perdue.

(8.) Susan Perdue.

(9.) Rebecca Ann Perdue.

29TH GENERATION.—(4.) Abi Hole, (May 16, 1788–Mar. 23, 1855.) married in 1808, to Peter Preston, sixth child of John and Rebecca Preston, who was born in Bedford County, Va., March 2, 1786, and died in Columbiana County, Ohio, Sept. 17, 1854. They lived near Lynchburg, Va., until June, 1825, when they removed to Columbiana County, O. They were both buried at Augusta Friends' Meeting House. To Abi Hole and Peter Preston were born sixteen children.

30TH GENERATION.—(1.) Charles Hole, born Feb. 27, 1809; died Dec. 14, 1844.

(2.) Martha Vickers, Sept. 28, 1810; died Oct. 7, 1843.

(3.) Mary Knight, born Dec. 31, 1811; died Dec. 5, 1881.

(4.) Edwin Thomas, born Mar. 14, 1813; died Feb. 9, 1902.

(5.) Elouisa, born Oct. 13, 1814; died May 18, 1861.

(6.) William Penn, born Jan. 14, 1816; died June 4, 1895.

(7.) Caleb Mead, born Nov. 22, 1817; died Dec. 9, 1883.

(8.) Sarah Ann, born April 23, 1819; died Mar. 24, 1895.

(9.) Hartwell Lyttleton, born June 20, 1821; died Dec. 12, 1889.

(10.) Junius Addison, born Dec. 29, 1822; died Oct. 23, 1897.

(11.) John Alexander, born Oct. 28, 1824; died Feb. 15, 1899.

(12.) Minerva Jane, born Sept. 25, 1826; died Oct. 4, 1893.

(13.) Eliza Rebecca, born June 20, 1828; died July 16, 1883.

(14.) Charlotte Elizabeth, born Jan. 7, 1830; living.

(15.) Lindley Murray, born Nov. 22, 1831; died Oct. 12, 1902.

(16.) Joseph Warren, born Aug. 21, 1834; died Feb. 15, 1837.

30TH GENERATION.—(1.) Charles Hole Preston, married Susan Hicklin and had issue, (1.) William Cullen, who died in Davenport, Iowa. (2.) Elvira Jane, died in Damascus, Ohio, and (3.) Charles H. Preston, living in Davenport, Iowa.

(2.) Martha Vickers Preston, married James Green, and had issue,

31ST GENERATION.—(1.) Edwin, died in infancy.

[2.] Samuel, died in Indiana, after marriage.

[3.] Charles Hole, married, deceased.

[4.] Caroline Frances, married Robert Grimes, both deceased.

[5.] William, died unmarried.

[6.] Alvan, married, has sons: Harry, Alva and Paul Green.

[7.] John, died aged 14.

[8.] James Edward, the only living child of Martha Green, resides in Matilijo, California, has one son John. (M. D.)

30TH GENERATION.—[3.] Mary K. Preston, married James Thompson. (born in England Oct. 20, 1804, died in Lisbon, Ohio, in 1898, aged 94.) Mary Thompson died at Lisbon, Ohio, Dec. 5, 1881, without issue.

30TH GENERATION.—(4.) Edwin Thomas Preston married Mary Jane Chambers and had issue,

31ST GENERATION.—(1.) William Selwyn, married, lives in Florida; has one daughter, (only living grandchild of Edwin Preston.)

(2.) Charles, married; no issue.

(3.) Abi, married John Knutting. No issue.

(4.) Junius W., never married, Baxter, Jasper County, Iowa.

(5.) Hartwell, never married.

(6.) Edward, unmarried.

(7.) George Albert unmarried.

(8.) Mary, died aged 6.

(9.) Caroline M., single, Baxter, Iowa.

30TH. GENERATION.—[5th.] Elouisa Preston, married John T. Johnson, and had issue one son, Preston Hill Johnson,unmarried, living.

[6th.] Dr. William Penn Preston, married Cynthia E. Tinker and had issue,

31ST. GENERATION.—[1st.] Annetta Mary, married John Smith and has issue Frank, Olive, and a younger son.

[2nd.] Olive Phebe, married Byron Elliott and has issue [1] Floy, [married Victor Eichol, Cleveland, O.]

31ST GENERATION.—[2nd.] William P. Elliott died in infancy.

31ST GENERATION.—[3rd.] Emma Van Gorder Preston, married Geneo Shaw, and has issue.

[1st.] Nellie Shaw, died unmarried, in Alliance, O.

[2nd.] Jessie Shaw, married Dr. Bretz, Cleveland, O.

[3rd.] Augusta Shaw, single, at home, 36 Jessie St., Cleveland. O.

31ST. GENERATION.—[4th.] Charles Preston, died in infancy.

Dr. William Penn Preston (see above.) 6th of the sixteen children of Abi and Peter Preston, was born near Lynchburgh, Virginia, and died in Alliance, Ohio, June 4th, 1895, lacking but 10 days of completing his 80th year. He came to Columbiana County, Ohio, with his parents in 1825 and began at a very early age, the study of medicine. He practiced at Augusta and Paris, O., till 1850 and removed to Mendota, Illinois. Upon the breaking out of the war he enlisted with an Illinois regiment as surgeon and remained in the service until the close of the war. In 1868 he removed to Alliance, O., where he practiced medicine until his death, having always a large and successful practice. Dr. Preston, while an eminent medical student and professional man, inclined toward literature and during his life wrote many articles and poems for the best magazines and newspapers of the country. He continued his literary labors until within a few weeks of his death. He had in his possession a large number of poems which have not yet been published. One of his last productions was a poem written for the Annual Old Folks' Party in September, 1894, which occasion he so deeply enjoyed. In Randolph, Ohio, Dr. Preston was married to Miss Cynthia E. Tinker, a most excellent, refined and lovely woman, who survives her husband, and now makes her home with her daughter, Mrs. Emma Shaw, at No. 36 Jessie street, Cleveland, Ohio. Dr. Preston was an active member of the Christian Church all his life, and for many years was an Elder in that denomination. He was an active advocate of temperance reform and his influence was always felt on the right side of reform movements. His death was the result of heart failure following a severe attack of the grippe.

[7.] Caleb Mead Preston, married Ann Eliza Morris, Nov. 19, 1846; (See Miller and Morris families, appendix.) had issue, four children.

31ST GENERATION.—[1.] A daughter, died in infancy.

[2.] Ella, died aged 6 years.

[3.] William Florydon, Congregational minister, married Lucy Wilson, and had issue seven children.

[4.] Charles Lyndon, married Della Reynolds who survives him and lives in Waldron, Mich., has a family.

30TH GENERATION.—[8.] Sarah Ann Preston, died near Lisbon, O., March 24, 1895, aged 76 years, never married.

[9.] Hartwell Lyttleton Preston, married in California, and died Dec. 12, 1889, leaving no children.

[10.] Junius Addison Preston, married Elizabeth Barcroft and had issue one son.

31ST GENERATION—Laurentius Sylvius, who married Emma ——, and had issue,

32ND GENERATION.—[1.] Minnie, married a Perry.

[2.] Ella, married Charles Rudesil and has issue, Frank Mabel, Vern and Earl.

(3.) Eunice, married Frank Gillett and has two children.

[4.] Jessie, married Joseph Youster.

[5.] Ralph Lee, unmarried.

[6.] Bertha, unmarried.

[7.] Lura, unmarried.

30TH GENERATION.—[11th.] John Alexander Preston, married Hannah Bentley and had issue seven children. Married 2nd, Emily Gray and had issue three children.

31ST GENERATION.—[1.] Laura Maria, married William Hall and had issue, Charles, Lyndon and Mabel.

[2.] Almeda E., married Lewis Penwell and had issue, Hartwell, [deceased.] Harry, married and lives in California; Ida died in childhood; Almeda Maria Penwell married [2nd.] Jack Mast and has issue Glen, Allie and Raymond.

[3.] Horace Bentley Preston, married Louie Richmond; has issue Nora, Gertie and Harry.

[4.] Charles Sumner Preston, married Rena Martin, has issue Lela, Carroll, Elloyda and Don.

[5.] Lindley Franklin Preston, married Tryphena Blackman, no issue.

[6th,] Mary Janette Preston, married Frank A. Wilson and has issue Harold Preston Wilson.

[7th.] Elmer E. Preston, married May McGilvary, and has Harley, Ethel and a younger daughter.

[8th.] Amy Vesta Preston, unmarried.

[9th.] William Everett Preston, unmarried.

[10th.] Olive May Preston, unmarried.

30TH. GENERATION.—[12th.] Minerva Jane Preston, married March 27, 1851,Thomas C. Morris [see Miller and Morris families Appendix] and had issue,

31ST. GENERATION.—(1st.) Adrienne Elouisa, died unmarried, March 27, 1895.

(2nd.) Luella Mary. married Stacy Wallace and has issue Ethel Wallace (address Washington D. C.)

(3rd.) Lindley Warren Morris, married Fanny May Darling, and had issue three children, Lindley, Warren, Hattie Darling, and Willis Hamilton,(deceased)

(4th.) Abbie Wilma, unmarried, Lisbon, O.

(5th.) Dr. William Ernest, married Flora Whitney.

(6th.) Eva Sophia, married Prof. Harvey Van Fossan, and has issue, Elaine, Ernest, Jean, Lindley Morris and Robert, New Lyme, Trumbull Co., Ohio.

30TH GENERATION.—(13.) Eliza Rebecca Preston, married Joseph B. Smith, and had issue,

31ST. GENERATION.—[1.] Lyndon Preston Smith, died, aged 9 years.

(2.) Hartwell Sumner, married Anna Fitzpatrick, and had issue, Mary K., Clara, Martha and Sarah, (deceased).

(3.) Willey Leander, married; has issue Lyndon.

(4.) Ulysses Grant Smith, married and lives in Cleveland, O., had issue, Frank, (deceased), Helen and Joseph.

(5.) Ledra Minerva, unmarried, Wheeling, W. Va.,

30TH GENERATION.—(14.) Charlotte Elizabeth Preston, married Rev. William Cope, March 8, 1870, had no children. Rev. William Cope died Feb. 8, 1892. His widow resides in Caro, Michigan, and adopted Frances Cope who married Ralph Geron and has issue one daughter, Viola Geron, who resides with her grandmother. Charlotte Elizabeth Cope, is the last surviving member of the large family of Abi and Peter Preston.

(15.) Lindley Murray Preston married Mattie Howe, no issue.

(16.) Joseph Warren Preston, the sixteenth child, died of inflammation of the brain at the age of 2½ years, Feb. 15, 1837.

JUDGE LINDLEY WARREN MORRIS.

See Generation XXX [12.] [3.] Judge Morris [with a twin sister, Louella Mary [Wallace] was born in Knox Township, Columbiana County, Ohio, October 16, 1853. While his father was in the Civil War the family resided in Damascus, Ohio, but with that exception his early years were spent on a farm. He was attending the New Lisbon High School, as a pupil of Prof. Israel P. Hole, [Generation XXX [3.] of Mahlon Hole] when, at the age of 16 years he was appointed and took oath as Deputy Sheriff of Columbiana County, under his father, Col. Thomas C. Morris, who held the office of Sheriff for two terms, 1870-1874. During all of this time and a part of the term of Col. Morris' successor in office, he acted as chief deputy and although under age and having only the experience of a farmer's boy and often called upon to act in matters requiring good judgment, tack and courage, no official act ever received criticism or censure. Having a taste for law and desiring to enter that profession he determined to complete a college course and accordingly entered Oberlin College in 1874, graduating in 1878. He then entered the office of the late Judge, W. A. Nichols, of Lisbon, Ohio, and was admitted to the bar of Ohio in May, 1880. In August, 1880 he began practice in Toledo, Ohio, and there continued till elected to the bench in 1893. Judge Morris was first named as a Republican candidate for the office of Judge of the Court of Common Pleas of the

1st Sub-district of the 4th Judicial District of Ohio, in 1889, and was defeated by less than 300 votes, though leading the Republican ticket. In 1893 he was nominated and elected, for the same district, consisting of Erie, Huron, Lucas, Ottawa and Sandusky Counties, by a plurality of 6700, for a term of 5 years, was re-elected in 1898, and at the election in Nov., 1903, was re-elected for a third term without any opposition, receiving a total of 29,323 votes, an unprecedented vote in that district. He was a member of the Common Council of Toledo from April, 1891 to Oct., 1894, when he resigned to take his seat on the bench. He was President of the Council for one term. His last election to the bench was without an opposing candidate, plainly showing the general satisfaction with which his excellent work has been received by the people in this large district. Judge Morris was married Dec. 27, 1894, to Miss Fannie May Darling, of Hyde Park, Boston, and is the father of three children: Lindley Warren Morris, Jr., born Oct. 28, 1895, Hattie Darling and Willis Hamilton [twins] born May 12, 1898. Willis Hamilton died May 14, 1898.

MAHLON HOLE'S FAMILY.

29TH GENERATION.—[7.] Mahlon Hole was born in Loudoun County, Va. He removed to Ohio at an early date and married Dec. 8th, 1819, Rachel Schooley, [daughter of Elisha Schooley, Apr. 23d, 1756—June 19th, 1838] [son of John and Mary Schooley] and Rachel [Holmes] Schooley [daughter of William and Mary Holmes,] born Apr. 17th, 1759, died July 18th, 1834. Mahlon and Rachel Hole began housekeeping in Salem, Columbiana Co., and afterwards removed to the farm near Augusta where they resided till the death of Mahlon, which occurred Mar. 13, 1871, aged, past seventy-eight years. Rachel Schooley Hole survived her husband for twenty-four years, and died at the age of 100 years and 6 months, at the home of her son, Prof. I. P. Hole, at Damascus Ohio. Rachel Hole, a beloved member of the family, yet not a Hole by birth, was cared for during the latter years of her life by her daughter Mary Hole, [now Mary Coulson] and by her daughter-in-law, Mary Miller Hole, wife of Prof. I. P. Hole. Her portrait given in this volume was taken by the writer when Rachel Hole, was in her 100th year. She was a woman of a remarkably fine mind and a striking and forceful personality. She retained her mental faculties almost completely to the end of her long and useful life. She is the fourth centenarian named in this book but the only one whose portrait can be presented. She was born near Leesburgh, Loudoun Co., Va., July 17th, 1794 and died Feb. 11th, 1895, was buried at the Friends' Meeting House near Augusta.

To Mahlon and Rachel Hole were born six children.

30TH GENERATION.—(1.) Charlotte, born April 26, 1822, married Jesse Kersey Pettit, (son of William Pettit, 1773–1849 and Mary Phipps Pettit, 1782–1843) born Oct. 24, 1819, died May 3d, 1902, and had issue,

31ST GENERATION.—(1.) Lucretia Pettit, born June 30, 1846, married Lunsford H. Bashaw (born March 25, 1844) March 22, 1871, and had issue,

32ND GENERATION.—(1.) Leon Hamlin Bashaw, born Dec. 18, 1871, married Jennie F. Cunningham, Nov. 1, 1897, and had issue,

33RD GENERATION.—Lucretia Isabell, born Aug. 24, 1898; Russell J. Bashaw, born Oct. 12, 1899. Leon married 2nd, Theresa Shriver.

32ND GENERATION.—(2.)—Leslie Dinsmore Bashaw, born Dec. 22, 1873, married Jan. 6, 1904, Lottie Smith, East Liverpool, O.

(3.) Raymond Odell Bashaw, born Oct. 24, 1876.

(4.) Alzada M. Bashaw, born Jan. 20, 1884.

31ST GENERATION.—(2.) Elmyra Pettit, born Aug. 30, 1848, died Oct. 13, 1863.

(3.) Jared H. Pettit, born Dec. 18, 1851, died unmarried, May 14th, 1902.

30TH GENERATION—(2.) Jared Hole, born Nov. 8, 1823, died March 20, 1850.

(3.) Israel P. Hole, born April 2, 1827, married Sept. 29, 1852, Mary Miller (see Miller family, appendix) died April 28, 1897; had issue 2 sons (twins.) [1] Mahlon Hole, born Feb. 3, 1861, died Sept. 26, 1873. [2] Morris J. Hole, born Feb. 3, 1861, married May 15, 1884, Eliza W. Spear, born March, 1860, and has issue,

32ND GENERATION.—[1.] Mahlon W. Hole, born July 21, 1886.

[2.] Morris Clifford Hole, born June 22, 1890.

30TH GENERATION.—[4.] Mary Hole, born March 14, 1829, married Benjamin Coulson, born Jan. 22, 1825, son of Jabez Coulson [Jan. 17, 1797-Feb. 14, 1886] son of John and Jane Coulson; and of Sarah Garrett, [June 23, 1733-July 31, 1850] daughter of Joseph and Charity Garrett, of Chester Co., Pa. Benjamin Coulson and Mary Hole were married Oct. 2nd, 1889, and reside at Whatcheer, Iowa.

(5.) Elisha Hole, born May 14, 1831; died Mar. 23, 1837.

(6.) Jacob Grinnell Hole, born Sept. 5, 1833; married Sophia Miller, (see Miller Family, appendix,) July 30, 1859, died June

27, 1864. Sophia Miller Hole was born Jan. 8, 1839; survived her husband, Jacob Grinnell Hole, and on Feb. 11, 1868, married Caleb Hole, son of John and Catherine. (Gen. XXX (5) Jacob and Sophia Hole, had issue, two children,

31ST GENERATION.—(1.) Judson G. Hole, born Dec. 8, 1862, died Oct. 26, 1864.

(2.) Charlotte Hole, born Aug. 9, 1860, married Mar. 18, 1885, Rev. Benjamin Farquhar, now of Whittier, California.

Professor Israel P. Hole, son of Mahlon and Rachel (Schooley) Hole, was born in Salem, Ohio, April 2, 1827. After working on his father's farm he entered Mt. Union College and received a liberal education. During his course in college he taught during the winter and became noted as a successful and thorough teacher. Thirty-five years of his life were devoted to educational work. Soon after leaving Mt. Union College, he, in connection with his brother Jacob, established Damascus Academy, of which institution he was the first principal, 1857 to 1860. He returned to the Academy as principal, in 1877, remaining with it until his retirement from school work in 1884. He was superintendent of the public schools of Lisbon, Salineville, Akron and Wellsville. He was a born educator, a ready and forcible speaker and a well-known lecturer upon scientific and economic subjects. As an educator he was thorough and progressive, endowed with large intellectual grasp and fine power of expression, together with great tenderness of heart and sympathy with the young. Prof. Hole was in politics, a Republican, and twice in congressional convention was a strong candidate for congressional nominee, being defeated by only a few votes. In religion he was a Friend and a prominent leader in Ohio Yearly Meeting. He married, Sept. 29, 1852 Mary Miller, (see Miller family, appendix,) who with one son, Morris J. Hole, survives him. Prof. Hole died suddenly, of heart failure, at his home near Damascus, Ohio, April 28, 1897, aged 70 years.

FAMILY OF NATHAN HOLE.

XXIX.—Nathan Hole was born in Bedford Co., Virginia, came with his parents to Columbiana Co., Ohio, in 1816, and on Oct. 28, 1818, married Sarah Armstrong, daughter of James and Ruth Armstrong, who was born September 22, 1793. Sarah Armstrong Hole died Feb. 20, 1870, and was survived by her husband only eight months, Nathan dying on Nov. 9, 1870; they had ten children.

XXX.—(1) Phebe Hole, born Aug. 23, 1819, married Joseph Cope; (born June 3, 1820, died June 11, 1879,) died July 2, 1894, had issue,

XXXI.—(1) Lycurgus C. Cope, married Eliza Grizell and had issue,

XXXII.—Sherman, Susie, William and Eva; Sherman married Lecia Stanley and has issue, Stanley and Verda.

XXXI.—(2) James C. Cope, married Mary H. Carter and had issue,

XXXII.—Bertha, Bernard and Florence, married to Err Williams and had one child, Grace Williams.

XXXI.—(3) Oliver Cope, married Mary E. Erwin and had issue,

XXXII.—Larwin Erwin, Alice and Laura.

XXXI.—(4) Lucina Cope, unmarried.

(5) Mary Cope, married Dio Rogers and had issue,

XXXII.—Phebe, Rufus, grand-children Raymond and Albert.

XXXI.—[6] Eliphez Cope married Emma Stewart. Childrens' names not given but has grand-children, Paul, Esther, Price, Louis, Joseph, Martha Berthil and Olney.

[7] Edith Cope, never married, deceased.

[8] Emmor Cope, married Rebecca Hoops, and had issue,

XXXII, Rollin and Clarence living; Lauretta and Elma deceased.

XXX.—[2] Ethan Hole, born Nov, 14, 1820, married Mary N. Cope, Mar. 18, 1842, who died Nov. 19, 1842. Married 2nd, Hannah Woods, July 16, 1846, who died March 2, 1890. Ethan Allen Hole died Nov. 23rd, 1878 at Canfield, Ohio. He was an eminent and successful physician, had issue by 1st wife, Mary N. now Mrs. Frank Cowden, of Palo Alto, California, born Nov. 19, 1842; by 2nd wife, Hannah, 1. Samuel J. Hole; 2. Sarah Ann Hole; 3. John Franklin Hole.

[3] Dr. James M. Hole, born June 14, 1822, married Aug. 13, 1841, Miss Hannah Baker who died Feb. 4, 1895. Dr. Hole died July 26, 1901, had issue.

XXXI.—[1] Dr. Linneaus Charles Hole, born May 30, 1847, died Sept. 4, 1888, married July 9, 1868, Rachel Painter, of Damascus, Ohio, and had issue, XXXII, 1. Sylvia R., born Nov. 16, 1869, and James M., 1871, died 1873. Sylvia R. Hole married Frank Evans in 1892, and had issue, Geneva Marie, born Feb. 28, 1898, died 1902. Mrs. Evans resides in Emporia, Kansas.

XXXI.—[2] Ruth Anna Hole, born Sept 2d, 1850, married Dec. 31, 1872 to John B. Park, has issue one son,

XXXII.—Frank H. Park, born May 7th, 1874, married July 19th, 1897, Anna Garwood and has issue, 3 children,

XXXIII.—[1] Louis Clifton, born Sept. 7th, 1898.

    [2] Alice Gertrude, born July 16th, 1900.

    [3] James Frederic, born Sept. 6th, 1901.

DR. JAMES M. HOLE.

Dr. Hole, born near Augusta, O., began the study of medicine in 1842, with Dr. R. Quegley of Calcutta, O., and later with Dr. Parker, of East Fairfield. He graduated from the Pennsylvania Medical College of Philadelphia, the Eclectic Medical University of Philadelphia, and the United States Medical College of N. Y. He began to practice in Salem, Ohio, in 1846. He subsequently became Professor of Theory and Practice in the Philadelphia University of Medicine and Surgery and afterwards in the St. Louis Eclectic Medical College. After resigning the latter professorship he again located in Salem where he resided and practiced until his death. Dr. Hole was the originator and prime mover of the Salem Electric Railway Company and was at one time its president. He was also one of the original promoters of the Columbiana County Pioneer Association. He was a regular writer for a number of medical journals in the U. S. He was generous to a fault and did many acts of kindness in a quiet way. Many persons received help from him. He was of a jovial disposition, a good entertainer and said by his patients to be as helpful in this way as was his medicine. He was devoted to his profession in Eastern Ohio. His son Dr. Linneaus Hole was graduated from the Philadelphia Dental College in 1865 and practiced dentistry in Salem until 1874, when he was graduated from the St. Louis Eclectic Medical College and practiced medicine in Salem for 13 years. In 1887 he went to Bon Aqua, Tenn. He died in Bon Aqua Sept. 4th, 1888. Dr. James M. Hole, died suddenly on July 26th, 1901, in the eightieth year of his age.

XXX.—[4] Jane Hole, born Mar. 31, 1824, married Nathan Cope, died at New Waterford, Ohio, Nov. 13, 1897, had issue ten children.

XXXI.—[1] James Byron Cope, born 1842, married Mary A. Gauger and has issue, 1. Tryverse, 2. Clarence, (deceased)

3. Carrie, (deceased), 4. Cora, married George Lower, 5. William and 6. Paul. Tryverse married Nettie Poulten and has Bessie, Earl, Brown and Clarence.

[2] Linda L. Cope, married James Kinnear and had issue,

[1] Frank C., married Maud Wilgus.

[2] Norma Cambia, married Rev. C. C. Chain and is deceased.

[3] Louisa M., married Robert Gray and had issue Noble N Gray, married to Margaret Stackoud, and had issue, Gay, Florence and Mabel Gray.

[4] Joseph Cope, born 1849, married Clara Denton and has issue, Sidney, Troy and Helen.

[5] John D. Cope, born 1851, married Louisa Guy, has issue, Charles, Raymond, Maggie and Paul.

[6] Allen B. Cope, born 1851, married Wilma Gauger and has issue, 1. Nettie, 2. Zula, 3. Zora, 4. Clara and 5. Bertha. 1. Nettie married Frank Johnson; 2, Zula married Edward Bloom; Nettie and Frank Johnson have issue, Evylin and Charlotte.

XXXI.—[7.] Franklin S. Cope, born 1855, married Jessie Rolli, no issue.

[8.] Charles Sumner Cope, born 1857, died Dec. 14, 1884.

[9.] Emma S. Cope, born 1859, married Emerson Dildine, no issue.

[10.] Mary E. Cope, born 1862, married James Phillips and has issue, Leeta Vivian and Hattie Lenore. Leeta Phillips married Thomas Casselman.

XXX.—[5.] Mary Hole, born Jan. 16, 1856, died unmarried.

[6.] Dr. Samuel Hole, born Aug. 29, 1827, (a twin), married in 1850, Rebecca Woods, and had issue,

XXXI.—[1.] Louisa R., New Waterford, O.

[2.] Emerson B., lives in Michigan.

[3.] William T., lives in Michigan.

[4.] Charles C., lives in Nebraska.

Dr. Samuel Hole, married second, Mary A. Endly, and had issue,

[5.] Laura R., married I. D. Barr, Irwin, Pa.

[6.] Jennie, married Frank Fessler, Beaver Falls, Pa.

[7.] Clarence A., lives in Hanover, Ohio.

[8.] Nathan J., lives in Wellsville, Ohio.

XXX.—[7.] Samuel's Twin, born Aug. 29, 1827; died Aug. 31, 1827.

(8th) Jacob Hole, born Oct. 23, 1829; died Jan. 18, 1830.

(9th) Joseph Hole, born Nov. 20th, 1830, died Feb. 8th, 1831

(10th) Sarah Hole, born Sept. 29th, 1832, married Samuel M. Roller, Nov. 3rd, 1853. Lives at Greenford, Ohio, had issue nine children.

31ST. GENERATION.—(1st.) Elvira J.,(Mrs. O. S. Walter), Greenford, Ohio.

(2nd) Melissa M., (Mrs. J. H. Calvin), Salem, Ohio.

(3rd) Arthur C. Roller, Columbiana, Ohio.

(4th) Anna L. Roller, (Mrs. J. D. Cook), Salem, Ohio.

(5th) Ida I. Roller, Greenford, Ohio.

(6th) Harry W. Roller, died May 31st, 1886.

(7th) Charles Jay Roller, Greenford, Ohio.

(8th) Ernest I. Roller, Greenford, Ohio.

(9th) Emma I. Roller, died Mar. 31st, 1872, (aged 2 years).

Samuel W. Roller, died Mar. 31st, 1922, aged 76 years.

FAMILY OF JONAH HOLE.

29TH GENERATION.—(9th) Jonah Hole, born in Bedford County, Va. in 1796. Married at Flushing, Belmont Co., O., on Mar. 27th, 1822, Elizabeth Ellis, who was born in Culpepper County, Va., Dec. 5th, 1797, (daughter of Jonathan and Lydia Ellis). Jonah Hole was a noted minister in the Friends Church,and traveled and preached throughout Canada, the Carolinas, New England and the Middle States. Jonah and Elizabeth Hole had five children, all born in Belmont Co., O. They removed to Champaign Co., in 1840 where Elizabeth died July 18th, 1843. Jonah died in Nov. 1862.

CHILDREN OF JONAH AND ELIZABETH (ELLIS) HOLE.

XXX.—(1) Lydia Ann, born Jan. 14th, 1823, married John Hunter Haines, had four children, died 1876, in Michigan.

XXXI.—(1) Arvine Preston Haines, 1848-1902, married Celinda Jason, have son Geo. P. Haines, 1872, of Grand Rapids, Mich.

(2) Rose Haines, 1850, married Geo. P. Jones and has son Lee Jones, 1873, Vandalia, Mich.

(3) Dr. Thomas J. Haines, M. D., 1853, married Blanche Moore. No issue. Three Rivers, Michigan.

(4) Anna B. Haines, 1857, married first, Isaac Hull and had Gena Hull, 1877, and Harry Hull, 1881, (married and has son) both of Chicago, Ill. Married second, Edward Lambur, of Elkhart, Indiana.

XXX.—(2) Mary R. Hole, born Jan. 28th, 1824, married Rev. Daniel W. Axline; resides in Lexington, Kentucky, had issue one daughter, Mary Ellen, deceased.

(3.) Jonathan Hole, born Dec. 13, 1825, married (1st) Susannah Hockett, and had issue, 4 children. (1) Francis Orlando, born May 23, 1853, married Mariah Bailey and had 2 children, Frank and Laura. Frank Hole lives in Wilmington, Ohio, (unmarried. Laura married a Mr. Hammer and lives in Springfield, O. (2) Florence Eva, born 23d Sept., 1854, married Emerson Moore and has son, Howard, Springfield. O. (3) Anna E. Hole, born Jan. 21, 1857, married Alonzo Larkin and lives in Highland County, Ohio. (4) Chas. E. Hole, born Nov. 11, 1859, single and lives in Boulder, Colorado.

Jonathan married (2nd) Jennette Heiler and has son, John Oliver, born Nov. 7, 1866, single and lives in San Francisco, Cal. Jonathan resides at No 2021 Mulberry, street, Muscatine, Iowa.

(4.) Elizabeth Hole, born Aug. 18, 1828, married Elliot Haines, and had one son, Charles W. Haines. Elizabeth and husband both deceased.

(5.) Dr. Jonah Hole, born April 6, 1831, married Aug., 1853, Margaret L. Rice [daughter of Louis and Eliza Rice. Louis Rice was son of Thomas Robert Rice, of Mass., who went to Virginia thence to Greenville, Tenn., thence to Eaton, Ohio, thence to Penelton, Ind., thence to Georgetown, Ill.] To Jonah and Margaret Hole were born eleven children, seven of whom are living, viz:

1. Louis W. Hole married Eva York; is postmaster at Ridge Farm, Ill.

2. Dr. Oliver C. Hole, of Danville, Ill., married Lucy Castle.

3. Chas. W. Hole, of Orange, Texas, general manager of the Orange and Northwestern R. R., married Margaret M. Williams and has son, Joseph Williams Hole, born July, 1892, in El Paso, Texas.

4. Dr. Frank M. Hole, Ridge Farm, Ill., married Rosa Williams.

5. Lydia Hole, married Evan J. Arnold, of Orlando, Florida.

6. Margaret L. Hole, married H. F. Gilkerson, Ridge Farm, Illinois.

7. Louisa J. Hole married Frank Pribble, Ridge Farm, Ill.

Dr. Jonah Hole and wife celebrated their golden wedding, Aug. 13, 1903. They reside in Ridge Farm, Illinois, where he practices dentistry with his son, Dr. F. M. Hole.

XXIX.—(10) Mary Hole born March 20th, 1798, died February 12th, 1883, married April 28th, 1825, John Green, born July 21st, 1792, died July 4th, 1884, had issue.

XXX.—(1) Thomas Green born May 12th, 1826, died April 22nd, 1894. Married January 1st, 1863, Nancy Niblock, born April 5th, 1835. No issue.

(2) Sophia Green, born October 23rd, 1827, died October 23rd, 1879. Married April 22nd, 1862, Thomas Hopkins, born June 21st, 1821, died February 28th, 1897, had issue,

XXXI.—(a) Mary Hopkins, born May 5th, 1863, died January 20th, 1886.

(b) Anna S. Hopkins, born June 29th, 1867, died Oct. 27th, 1900, married C. S. Moore.

XXXII.—(1) (a) Harold, born Nov. 3rd, 1896.

(b) Edith Mary, born March 24th, 1898, died Sept. 28th, 1898.

(c) Helen Anna, born June 24th, 1900.

XXX.—(3) Rachel Green, born May 15th, 1830, died Nov. 6th, 1902. Married Nov. 18th, 1868, William S. Wherry, born April 20th, 1832, died April 2nd, 1886, and had issue,

XXXI.—(a) Jno. G. Wherry, born July 31st, 1870, D. D. S., Elyria, Ohio.

(b) Mary Jeanette, born Sept. 12th, 1871, Elyria, Ohio.

(c) Olive Maud, born Aug. 7th, 1874, Elyria, Ohio.

XXX —(4) John H. Green, born June 16th, 1832, married Oct. 29th, 1862, Hannah Terrell, had issue,

XXXI.—(a) Mabel A., born July 2nd, 1865, married July 18th, 1883 Elmer H. White.

XXXII.—(a) Harold J., born July 16th, 1889.

(b) Lawrens, born June 12th, 1891, died Aug. 14th, 1893.

(c) Donald G., born Aug. 3rd, 1889.

XXXI.—(b) Clara R. Green, born Dec. 28th, 1866, married June 20th, 1894, Samuel T. Gray.

XXXII.—(a) Carl S., born April 16th, 1895.

    (b) Hugh G., born Oct. 11th, 1898.

    (c) Mabel E., born Feb. 12th, 1901.

    (d) Loren Thomas, born Aug 28th, 1902.

XXXI.—(c) Frank T. Green, born April 12th, 1870, married July 18th, 1900, Mabel E. Lyon.

XXXII.—(1) (a) Evelyn Luverne, born April 29th, 1901.

XXX.—[5] Mary T. Green, born May 27, 1834, married March 28, 1861, Peter L. Thomas, died February 16, 1890.

XXXI.—[a] Walter, born Dec. 10, 1863, married Dec. 28, 1892, Hannah L. Hunt.

    [b] Marianna, born Sept. 17, 1867, married Oct. 24, 1889, Rev. Truman C. Kenworthy.

XXXII.—[a] Helen, born July 8, 1890.

    [b] Mary, born May 31, 1892.

    [c] Richard, born April 14, 1894.

    [d] Catharine, born Jan. 3, 1898.

    [e] Eunice, born Oct. 24, 1899.

    [f] Isabel, born Oct. 3, 1902.

XXXI.—[c] Eleanor G., born April 12, 1870, married Dec. 18, 1894, George Ernest Kent.

XXXII.—[a] Arthur T., born Oct. 8, 1895.

    [b] R. Howard, born June 14, 1897.

    [c] Edith Edna, born Oct. 30, 1899, died Sept. 5, 1900.

XXXI.—[d] Esther H., born January 24, 1873.

XXX.—[6] Jacob A. Green, born Sept. 24, 1836, married Jan. 30, 1868, Martha Johnson, born July 20, 1839, issue,

XXXI.—[a] John E., born March 31, 1869, married Oct. 10, 1894, Alice Patterson, born July 22, 1869.

XXXII.—[a] John Jacob, born Oct. 20, 1898.

    [b] Robert, born May 30, 1901.

XXXI.—[b] Benjamin J., born Dec. 18, 1870, County Surveyor Harrison Co., Ohio.

[c] Mary, born April 19, 1875, married May 11, 1898, James Walter Grimes, born Oct. 20, 1869.

XXXII.—[a] Sara, born February 12, 1900.

[b] James Walter, Jr., born Nov. 30, 1902.

XXXI.—[d] Elizabeth, born Oct. 20, 1876, married March 23, 1899, Howard J. Holloway, born April 21, 1875.

XXX.—[7] James Green, born Nov. 6, 1838, died March 14, 1839.

[8] Abigial Green, born Jan. 30, 1840, died Feb. 19, 1846.

[9] Rebecca Green, born May 4, 1844, married May 28, 1868, Enoch Lewis, born May 5, 1838.

XXXI.—(2) (a) Mary H., born July 7, 1869.

(b) Alice G., born Oct. 10, 1871.

(c) John Frederick, born June 29, 1874, died Feb. 6, 1876.

(d) Charles S., born Jan. 16, 1877.

(e) George Henry, born Oct. 13, 1879.

(f) Esther, born Feb. 6, 1882.

(g) Austin F., born July 26, 1885.

(h) Walter E., born October 24, 1887.

JACOB HOLE'S FAMILY.

XXIX.—[11.] Jacob, the eleventh child of Jacob Hole and Mary Thomas, married Ann Chambers in 1828. She was the daughter of James Chambers, (born March, 1782, son of Thomas and Jane Chambers, of Ireland), and his wife Mary Nicholson, (daughter of James and Jane Nicholson, of Rickhill, Ireland, born Jan. 21, 1784), Ann, the oldest of their ten children, was born in Ireland Sept. 28, 1807, and died April 27, 1890, aged 83 years. Jacob Hole died at Butler Station, Indiana, March 14, 1873. Jacob and Ann Hole had issue, ten children,

XXX.—[1] William Hole, born Nov. 14, 1829, married Matilda Hasley, 1853; died 1891, had issue, seven children.

XXXI.—[1] Anna M. Hole, married Samuel Hamilton.

[2] Charles Hole, died in infancy.

[3] Willets J. Hole, married Mary G. Weeks.

[4.] Charles Hole.

[5] Joseph M. Hole, married Blanche McLaughlin.

[6] Laura E. Hole, married Marcellus Stearns.

[7] Walter M. Hole.

XXXII.— Frank J., Laura E., Charles A. and Walter N., children of (1) Anna and Samuel Hamilton.

Agnes M., daughter of Willets J. and Mary E. Hole.

Imogine, daughter of Joseph and Blanche Hole, died in infancy.

Howard O., Marcella H., Albert C., children of Marcellus and Laura Stearns.

XXX.—(2nd) Jonah W. Hole, born Jan. 22nd, 1831, married in 1863 Mary E. Sisson. No issue.

(3rd) James Hole, born Dec. 30, 1832, married Fannie Walker in 1858, have issue.

XXXI.—(1st) Edward W. Hole.

(2nd) Mollie L. Hole, married Samuel Conboy, and has son Marion Conboy.

XXX.—(4th) Charles Hole, born Nov. 23, 1834, died Aug. 5, 1842.

(5th) Thomas Hole, born Feb. 24, 1837, died Aug. 3, 1842.

(6th) John Hole, born June 9, 1839, died Aug. 4, 1842.

(7th) Joshua Hole, born Sept. 21, 1841, died an infant.

(8th) Mary Ellen Hole, born June 22, 1843, married Frank M. Leeds in 1868 and had issue,

XXXI.—(1st) Ella Leeds, married Randall Abrams.

(2nd) Owen Leeds, died in infancy.

(3rd) Jennie Leeds, died in childhood.

XXX.—(9th) Rebekah J. Hole, born Dec. 28, 1845. Married in 1867, Oscar N. Cowell and had issue, 8 children.

XXXI.—(1st.) Ella Cowell, died in infancy.

[2nd] Joseph Cowell, died in childhood.

[3rd] Frank Cowell.

[4th] Lora Cowell, married Jesse Donaldson, has daughter, Adelaide.

[5th] Myrtle Cowell, died in childhood.

[6th] Carrie Cowell, died in childhood.

[7th] Emma Cowell.

[8th] Charles Cowell, died in childhood.

XXX.—[10th] Joseph H. Hole, born Aug. 3, 1848, married in 1870, Lora Patrick, and had issue,

XXXI.—[1st]   Fred E. Hole, married Alice E. Rogers, has son Roger.

[2nd]   Bertha A. Hole, married Archie D. Stewart, has sons Paul, Harold and Donald H.

[3rd]   Ada M. Hole.

[4th]   Lena M. Hole.

CHAPTER XIII.

DESCENDANTS OF CHARLES HOLE AND ESTHER HANNA.

19TH GENERATION. (1) Charles Hole, eldest son of Jacob and Mary (Thomas) Hole, was married to Esther Hanna, May 16, 1811. After the preliminaries required by the Discipline of the Society of Friends, they were married at the time and place named in the following interesting document.

"Whereas, Charles Hole, of Middleton Township, in the County of Columbiana and State of Ohio, son of Jacob Hole, of Bedford County, State of Virginia, and Mary, his wife; and Esther Hanna, daughter of Robert Hanna, of Middleton Township, Columbiana County, Ohio, and Catharine, his wife, having declared their intentions of marriage with each other, before a monthly meeting of the religious Society of Friends held at Middleton according to the good order used among them, and having consent of parents, their said proposal of marriage was allowed by said meeting. Now these are to certify whom it may concern, that for the full accomplishment of their said intentions, this sixteenth day of the fifth month, in the year of our Lord, one thousand, eight hundred and eleven, they, the said Charles Hole and Esther Hanna, appeared in a public meeting of the said people held at the meeting house of Friends south of little Bull Creek, and the said Charles Hole taking the said Esther Hanna by the hand, did openly declare that he took her, the said Esther Hanna, to be his wife, promising with divine assistance to be unto her a loving and faithful husband until death should separate them; and then, in the same assembly, the said Esther Hanna did in like manner, declare, that she took him, the said Charles Hole, to be her husband, promising, with divine assistance, to be unto him a loving and faithful wife, until death should separate. And, moreover, they, the said Charles Hole and Esther Hanna [she according to the custom of marriage, assuming the name of her husband], did, as a further confirmation thereof, then and there to these presents set their hands.

Recorded,   CHARLES HOLE,
                                           ESTHER HOLE.

And we whose names are also hereunto subscribed, being present at the solemnization of said marriage and subscription, have, as witnesses thereto, set our hands the day and the year above written."

"William Underwood,	Robert Hanna,
Benjamin Scott,	Catherine Hanna,
John Edmundson,	Nathan Hole,
Susannah Heacock,	Ann Hole,
Sarah Heacock,	Tace Hole,
Amy Morlan,	Ury B. Hole,
Jane McMillan,	Catharine Hanna, Jr.
Jonathan Marsh,	Ann Hanna,
Sarah Thompson,	Robert Hanna, Jr.
Silvanus Fisher,	Anne Hanna,
Sarah Richardson,	Mary Morlan,
Sarah Scott,	Thomas Hanna,
Elizabeth Scott,	Benjamin Hanna.
Benjamin Samms,	Rachel Hanna,
James Marsh,	Joshua Hanna,
Edith Marsh,	Jason Morlan,
Ann Edmundson,	Joseph Fisher, Jr."

Charles and Esther Hole spent all the years of their married life in Columbiana County, Ohio. Esther was a minister in the Society of Friends and travelled extensively in Ohio and Virginia. She was a pioneer Anti-slavery advocate, laboring in this reform amongst the slave holders of Virginia. She was always courteously received by them and argued her cause where none but such a gentle and re_fined Quaker lady might dare approach such a subject.

From the Friends' Review 1st month, 5th, 1850. "Died, at the residence near Clarkson, Columbiana County, Ohio, on the 6th of last month. Esther, wife of Charles Hole, a minister and member of Carmel Monthly Meeting, in the fifty-eighth year of her age. During her last sickness, which was severe, she was remarkably favored with calmness and resignation, remaining sensible to the last." Charles Hole died June 23rd, 1854, and both were buried at Carmel Meeting House, Columbiana County, Ohio. To Charles and Esther Hole were born nine children.

XXX.—[1] Thomas Hole, born Jan. 2, 1812; died Oct. 30, 1869.

[2] Rebecca Hole, born Nov. 13, 1813; died Nov. 29, 1889.

[3] Catharine Hole, born Jan. 25, 1816; died July 31, 1894.

[4] Mary Ann Hole, born July 3, 1818; died Jan. 18, 1833.

[5] Benjamin Hole, born Oct. 25, 1820; died Feb. 3, 1903.

[6] Joseph Hole, born July 26, 1823; died April 27, 1887.

[7] Robert Hole, born Nov. 4, 1825; died Feb. 27, 1899.

[8] Jacob Hole, born July 18, 1828, Salem, Ohio.

[9] Hannah Hole, born April 10, 1832; died April 10, 1887.

XXX.—(1) Thomas Hole, born Jan. 2, 1812, died Oct. 30, 1869, married Abigail F. Moore, born March 6, 1821, died Sept. 15, 1894. Married Oct. 7, 1841.

CHILDREN OF THOMAS AND ABIGAIL HOLE.

Charles Virgil Hole, born Aug. 27, 1845, died Aug. 28, 1858.

George Alpine Hole, born Aug. 27, 1847.

Mary Hole, born Dec. 10, 1848, died Nov. 22, 1854.

Anna M. Hole, born Jan. 6, 1862.

Thomas Harvey Hole, born June 22, 1863.

M. E. Farr, married Anna M. Hole, July 4, 1876.

CHILDREN OF M. E. AND ANNA FARR.

Mary Annetta Farr, born Jan. 28, 1878.

Vergil H. Farr, born July 31, 1879.

Robert L. Farr, born Nov. 25, 1881.

Florence Farr, born Feb. 15, 1885.

Harold T. Farr, born Sept. 13, 1888.

Raymond Farr, born May 12, 1891, died Oct. 24, 1891.

Clarence L. Farr, born Aug. 13, 1895.

Donald Farr, born March 22, 1899.

Thomas Harvey Hole, Sarah Robinson married Mar. 17, 1886.

CHILDREN OF HARVEY AND SARAH HOLE.

George Willis Hole, born May 5, 1887.

Ethel Hole, born Feb. 25, 1889.

Eva Tamar Hole, born Jan. 7, 1892.

Esther Hole, born June 25, 1894.

Louis Marcus Hole, born Sept. 21, 1896.

Bertha Anna Hole, born Dec. 6, 1898,

Robert Vergil Hole, born Jan. 22, 1901.

XXX.—(2) Rebecca Hole, born Nov. 13, 1813, died Nov. 29th, 1839 married Israel Heald, (born Jan. 11th, 1807, died Jan. 25, 1888,) had issue seven children

XXXI.—(1) Ezra Heald, born Aug. 24, 1843, married Delita M. Crespin, Aug. 30th, 1877, and has Ida R., born Aug. 24th, 1878, and Walter E., Nov. 8th, 1882.

(2) Lydia A. Heald, born Feb. 2nd, 1845, died Oct. 8th, 1859.

(3) Mary Ann Heald, born Sept. 12th, 1846, married Samuel Embree, born Sept. 13th, 1842, and had issue nine children.

XXXII.—(1) Esther Rebecca, born July 9th, 1869.

(2) Myra Hannah, born Feb. 9th, 1871.

(3) Cynthia Heald, born Dec. 19th, 1872.

(4) Caroline E., July 13th, 1875, married Arthur H. Mott, May 21st, 1900, and had issue Ervin Lester Mott, born Nov. 3, 1902.

(5) Isabella Embree, born Sept. 17th, 1877.

(6) Elizabeth T., born Feb. 7th, 1880, died Aug. 25th, 1881.

[7] Edna Lydia, born Mar. 21st, 1882.

[8] Mary Irene, born June 14th, 1884.

[9] Warren Jesse born Sept. 29th, 1887.

XXXI.—[4] Lindley Heald, born March 25th, 1848, married Nancy L. Fritchman, Dec. 6th, 1871, and has issue three children.

XXXII.—[1] Edith L., born Oct. 30th, 1872, married Louis W. Emmons, May 6th, 1903.

[2] Margaret A., born July 20th, 1874.

[3] Lydia A., May 7th, 1883, married Roy R. Sheets, Dec. 23rd, 1903.

XXXI.—[5] Esther Heald, born March 13, 1850; died Sept. 21, 1852.

[6] Cynthia L., born March 3, 1852; died May 19, 1876.

[7] Charles, born April 25, 1854; died April 2, 1855.

XXX.—[3] Catherine Hole, born Jan. 25, 1816; died July 31, 1894. Married Nathan Engle, (born June 13, 1814; died Nov. 14, 1891,) in Jan. 1840, and had issue, seven children.

XXXI.—[1] Lemuel Engle, married Nancy Waller, and had issue,

[1] Lillian C., married Charles Leicht, deceased.

[2] Harvey R., married Visa Povle, died leaving issue Roy L. and May.

[3] Minnie H., married Edward Matheny, has issue Earl L,

XXXI.—[2] Esther, married James Crum, is deceased, leaving issue Arthur J., Edgar and Irwin J. Crum.

[3] Robert, married Sarah McQueety, and had issue, Charles, Mary and Queeta.

[4] Charles, married Sarah Cooper and died 1894, leaving issue, Robert, Ernest (married a Povle), and Mabel, who married Adeliza Davis, and has Herbert.

[5] Mary Elma, married John Crosand, and has Linton, Albert and Clarence.

[6] Eliza A., married Isaac Lindley, and has,

[1] Adelbert, married Ella Newsom, and has Ralph, Chester and Nettie.

[2] Virgil.

[3] Esther.

[7th] Albert N. Engle.

XXX.—MARY ANN HOLE, born July 3, 1818; died at Carthage, Ind., Jan. 18, 1883. Married at Carmel Meeting House, Columbiana Co., Ohio, on Dec. 26, 1844, to Aaron Huestis. Aaron Huestis, died in Nebraska.

CHILDREN OF AARON AND MARY ANN HUESTIS.

[1st] Isadora, died at Carthage, Ind.

[2nd] Samantha, died at Bridgeport, Ind., Dec. 2, 1893.

[3rd] Moses Henry, living at Cortland, Neb., in 1899, has two sons.

[4th] Emmor Benjamin, died at Bridgeport, Ind., July 3, 1872.

[5th] Charles H., pastor of Congregational Church at Exeter, Neb., in 1897. Has two children.

(5) Benjamin Hole, born in Columbiana Co., Ohio, Oct. 25, 1820; died at Fairland, Shelby Co., Ind., Feb. 3, 1903. Married in Jackson Co., Ind., June 17, 1857, to Isabel Wilson, who was born in Washington Co., Ind., Aug. 23, 1837.

CHILDREN OF BENJAMIN AND ISABEL W. HOLE.

XXXI.—(1) Myra Hannah, born in Jennings Co., Ind., Oct. 9, 1860, married at Bridgeport, Marion Co., Ind., Sept. 28, 1881, to Robert McBeth, who was born at Fraserburgh, Scotland, Oct. 24, 1851. Robert McBeth died at Fairland, Shelby Co., Ind., June 10, 1902.

(2) Charles Wilson, born at Bridgeport, Marion Co., Ind. Jan. 4, 1865, died at Bridgeport, Marion Co., Ind., July 18, 1865.

(3) *Allen David, born at Bridgeport, Marion Co., Ind., Aug. 6, 1866.

[4] Wilson Joseph, born at Bridgeport, Marion Co., Ind., April 23, 1868, married at Bridgeport, Marion Co., Ind., July 10, 1894, to Alfaretta Hoffman, who was born at Bridgeport, Marion Ind., Dec. 23, 1873.

[5] Rebecca Mary, born at Bridgeport, Marion Co., Ind., Feb. 2, 1870; died Oct. 12, 1870.

CHILDREN OF XXXI (4) WILSON JOSEPH AND ALFARETTA HOFFMAN HOLE.

1 Wymond W., born at Maryville, Tenn., July 2, 1895.

2 Maurice K., born in Marion Co., Ind., Nov. 9, 1896; died July 19, 1897.

3 Christine, born in Marion Co., Ind., June 6, 1898.

4 Russell C., born in Marion Co., Ind., April 3, 1900.

5. Carroll Hoffman, born in Bartholomew County, Indiana, Nov. 7, 1901.

XXX.—(6) Joseph Hole, son of Charles Hole and Esther Hanna Hole, born July 26, 1823; died April 27, 1887, married Nov. 26, 1846, Esther M. Pyle, daughter of Benjamin Pyle and Elizabeth Wright Pyle, born Nov. 29, 1823; died Dec. 21, 1898. Their children were:

1 Henrie Pyle Hole, born May 10, 1849; died, June 2, 1902.

2 Evelyn, born Jan. 6, 1852.

3 Elizabeth C., born Dec. 12, 1854.

4 Charles Fremont, born Aug. 4, 1856.

5 Linda Hannah, born Jan. 2, 1861.

6 Ella Mary, born Apr. 10, 1863.

7 and 8. Two children died in infancy.

*Prof. Allen D. Hole of Earlham College, Indiana, (see portrait) after some work in common schools, taught in high schools as follows: Friendswood Academy, Wisconsin, 1885-1887; Maryville Normal and Preparatory School Maryville, Tennessee 1894-95; Union High School, Westfield, Ind., 1898; Sand Creek Seminary, Azalia, Indiana, 1898-1900. Received his degree of Bachelor of Science from Earlham College, Richmond, Ind., in 1897. Received degree of Master of Arts from same college, in 1901. Since 1900 he has been a member of the Faculty of Earlham College, being at the present time Secretary of the Faculty and Professor of Geology. For the past three summers, 1901-'02 and '04 he has been enrolled in the graduate school of the University of Chicago for work in Geology. In pursuance of this work he spent the summer of 1903 in the Bighorn Mountains of Northern Wyoming.

XXXI.—[1st] Henrie P. Hole, married (first) Emma L. Appling, Oct. 30th, 1880.

Emma L. Hole, died June 18th, 1891. Their children are:

Albert George, born Nov. 5th, 1881.

Frank Rufus, born Dec. 11th, 1883.

Myrtle Luella, born May 15th, 1836.

Fredrick Harrison, born Sept. 24th, 1888.

Henrie P. Hole, married (second) Estella R. Child, June 5th, 1894.

[3] Elizabeth Hole, unmarried.

[2] Evelyn Hole, married Emmor C. Malmsbury, Feb. 22nd, 1873. Their children:

Frank B., born Jan. 21st, 1874.

Ida H., born May 22nd, 1876.

Clyde H., born June 19th, 1878.

Frank B., married Mamie Hairston, April 25th, 1900, and had issue, one child, Gladys, born June 7th, 1901.

Clyde H., married Mary A. Lindsey, Nov. 7th, 1902.

(4) Charles F. Hole, married Sarah Ryan, Sept. 15, 1896. Their children are:

Ruth, born Dec. 30, 1897.

Esther E., born June 23, 1899.

(5) Linnie H., married George M. Swarthout, Nov. 2, 1887. Children are:

Ella Harriet, born July 10, 1888.

Grace Evelyn, born June 14, 1891.

(6) Ella M., married Landon M. Kibler, May 15, 1902. One child:

Kirk Matson, born July 2, 1903.

XXX —(7) Robert Hole, born Nov. 4, 1825; married Caroline Morlan, daughter of Mordecai and Eliza Morlan*, Dec. 30, 1852, and
resided in Salem, Ohio, from that time until his death, which
occurred Feb. 27, 1899. He was a prominent and useful citizen
of Salem, serving on the School Board for 15 years and for 12

*Mordacai Morlan, son of Stephen Morlan and Mary, his wife, was born
May 11, 1743; married May 31, 1821, to Eliza Ann Dean, [daughter of Jonathan
R. and Hannah Dean], who was born Jan. 26, 1801. Mordacai and wife had
eleven children of whom Caroline who married Robert Hole, was the sixth,
and Amelia, who married Jacob Hole, was the tenth.   Albert M. the young :-
est child was born Oct. 10 1850 when his mother was 50 years old, and t e
event was considered "wellnigh miraculous" by the *wise women* of that day.

years of that time was the president. Though born a Friend, or Quaker, he identified himself with the Methodist Church and was for many years a trustee of the Salem M. E. Church. In politics, Robert Hole was, in early life, a Whig, but joined the Republican party at its formation. He joined the Masonic order and was one of the charter members of Salem Commandery No. 42, K. T. To Robert and Caroline Hole, were born eight children:

XXXI.—(1) Esther Hannah, born June 14, 1854; died Jan. 24, 1877.

(2) Walter M., born May 17, 1857; Salem, Ohio.

(3) Warren Watson, born Nov. 9, 1858; Salem, Ohio.

(4) Charles Dean, born May 23, 1860; Salem, Ohio.

(5) Marion Lenhart, born Sept, 9, 1864; Salem, Ohio.

(6) Willis Robert, (_twins_) born Sept. 15, 1866; Lisbon, O.
(7) Louis Jacob,) born Sept. 15, 1866; Del Norte, Col.

(8) Vesta Gertrude, born Nov. 9, 1871; died Aug. 10, 1873.

XXXI.—(2) Walter M. Hole. married Susie Earle (born June 1, 1860), and has issue, 1. Esther Gertrude, born Oct. 14, 1886 and 2. Henry Earle born Nov. 18, 1891.

XXXI.—(3) Warren Watson Hole, married July 10, 1884, Martha Eliza Whittlesey, born Oct. 20, 1857,* and had issue,

(1) Frederick Louis, born April 30, 1887.

*The Whittlesey family are of the family of William Whittlesey. Archdeacon of Huntingdon, elected 2,rd October, 1350; confirmed by the Pope 31st July, 1361; consecrated 18th Bishop of Rochester, February 1361; transferred to Worcester and consecrated Bishop of Worcester; appointed 57th Archbishop of Canterbury by King Edward III, crowned metropolitan and primate of all England, who stood next to the Pope in Romish hierarchy. Archbishop Whittlesey died at Lambeth Palace, Jan. 6, 1374. 1. John Whittlesey, born July 4, 1623, in Cambridgeshire, England, [son of John, born 1593], came to America in 1635; married Ruth Dudley, and died April 15, 1704, had issue 12 children, of whom the 12th. 2. Rev. Samuel Whittlesey, born 1686, married July 1, 1712, Sarah Chauncey, born 1688 who died Oct 23, 1767, died April 15, 1752. [Sarah Chauncey was the granddaughter of Rev. Charles Chauncey, of Yardly, England, born 1592, came to Mass. in 1 cc 1637, was the second president of Harvard College, died Feb. 19, 1682; married Catharine Eyre born 1614, died 1667, daughter of Robert Eyre of rerum. born 1594; married Anne, daughter of Rev. John Still Bishop, of Bath and Wells 1592, who married in 1593 Lady Jane Horner, born 1 5t daughter of Sir John Horner, Knight, and Lady Anne Speke, daughter of Sir George Speke, Knight.] Samuel and Sarah Whittlesey 2. had issue, with others, 8. Elisha Whittlesey, born Oct. 14, 1721, died Feb. 25, 1803; married April 8, 1754, Susannah Hall, had issue, with others, 4. Elisha, born Jan. 1, 1755; died Sept. 16, 1842; married Sept. 8, 1777, Sarah Jones and had issue, with others, 5. John Hall Whittlesey, born June 1, 1778, married Aug. 4, 1804, Charity Brush, and had issue, 6. John B. Whittlesey, born Aug. 15, 1805, married Emeline Mix; died in 1894 aged 94 years, had issue, 7. Charles Chauncey, born April 7, 1832; married June 1854 Sarah A. Shilling, [born April 4, 1833] died Oct. 1865, had issue, 8. Martha Eliza Whittlesey, born Oct. 20, 1857, married July 10, 1884 to Warren Watson Hole, as above. See portrait of Martha Whittlesey Hole, page 105.

(2)   Robert Whittlesey, born April 12, 1889, died Aug. 14, 1890.

(3)   Leonard Schilling, born Nov 29, 1893.

(4)   Edith, born Aug. 12, 1895.

XXXI.—(4) Charles Dean Hole, married June 14, 1890, Nellie Burwell, and has issue,

(1)   Caroline M., born May 29, 1891.

(2)   Elsie Dean, born Aug. 21, 1892.

(3)   Lawrence Robert, born Feb. 11, 1894.

(4)   Katharine E., born April 14, 1900.

(5)   Margery, born Aug. 4, 1901, died in infancy.

XXXI.—(5) Marion Lenhart Hole, married June 22, 1888, Emma Fawcett.

XXXI.—(6) Willis Robert Hole, married May 7, 1891, Elma Gilbert and has

(1)   Louis G., born July 6, 1892.

(2)   Robert J., born April 16, 1894.

(3)   Ernest M., born March 28, 1896.

XXXI.—(7th) Rev. Louis Jacob Hole, Sept. 15, 1866, married July 5th, 1893, Cora S. Burford, is at present pastor of the M. E. Church at Del Norte, Colorado. Had issue,

(1st)   Dorothy Hole, born Jan., 1895, died Nov., 1897.

(2nd)   Francis Hole, born Sept. 30, 1897.

(4th)   Hilda Hole, born Nov. 27, 1899.

Rev. Louis J. Hole was educated at the Salem Public Schools, and at Mt. Union College. He has always been considered the artist of the family and for some years worked along art lines, being with an Engraving Co., of Philadelphia and in the draughting dept., of the Mullin's Sheet Metal Statuary works of Salem, O. He felt called to the ministry and was licensed and afterwards ordained as a minister of the M. E. Church. His first charge was at Melbourne, Florida, where he continued to exhibit his love of art by making sketches of the tropical scenery of that region, which were published in a small but beautiful volume in 1895. Two of these sketches are here reproduced, without the consent of the artist himself, but by permission and concurrence of the family.

Since leaving Florida his pastorates have all been in Colorado, where he finds the climate favorable to his health, which was affected by asthma when he resided in lower altitudes. He has been stationed successively at Wray, Del Norte and Pagosa Springs, and is now preaching at Basalt. As a pastor he has always been beloved by his people and his labors have been crowned with abundant success, to which his ability to "talk with chalk" has contributed in no small degree.

HON. WARREN WATSON HOLE was born in Salem, Columbiana Co., Ohio, November ninth, 1858. He graduated from the Salem High School in June, 1876. He entered Mount Union College, and by taking extra studies, completed the course, and graduated on July twenty-fifth, 1878. He was the class poet and wrote the song which was sung by the class on commencement day. He studied law in the office of Kennett and Ambler at Salem, Ohio, teaching school in the winter; and also during his study of the law, from August, 1881 until March, 1882, acted as assistant Business Manager of the "Chautauquan" at Meadville, Pennsylvania.

He was admitted to the bar by the Supreme Court at Columbus, Ohio, in June. 1882, taking first rank in a class of forty-two. He enjoyed a large practice in the courts of his own state, and was counsel in a number of important cases, argued before the Supreme Court of Pennsylvania.

In April, 1884 he became Solicitor of the incorporated village of Salem and served for four years. He had charge of the legal steps, by which the village was raised to the class of a city and afterward served for four years. He was elected Judge of the court of common pleas, of the ninth judicial district of Ohio, in November, 1899, for a term beginning November first, 1900.

In February, 1900, Judge P. N. Smith resigned, and Governor Nash appointed Judge Hole to fill out the unexpired term. He has presided at the trial of many important cases in various counties of the district, and his decisions have generally been affirmed by the higher courts.

Judge Hole has always taken great interest in the religious, educational, social and political life of the community. He is a member and trustee of the Methodist Episcopal Church, and for a number of years was President of the Young Men's Christian Association. He is a member of the Board of Trustees of the Salem Public Library and was a member of the Board of Examiners of the Salem public schools for fifteen years, resigning when taking his place on the bench.

For many years he has been a member of the Masonic Order and at present is affiliated with Perry Lodge, number 185, Salem Chapter number 94, Salem Commandery, number 42, and Omega Council of Salem, Ohio. He is also a member of the Benevolent Protective Order of Elks. He is considered a most excellent toastmaster and after-dinner talker. Judge Hole has always taken an active interest in the welfare of the Republican party, in the city, county and state, and from the time he left college to his elevation to the bench, his voice has been heard in every campaign. Judge Hole is six feet, two inches in height, and weighs two hundred and twenty pounds. He is an enthusiastic hunter, and in college and since has taken great interest in athletics, and as a pedestrian has few equals. On July tenth, 1884, he was married to Martha E. Whittlesey. Four children have been born to them, of whom three are still living. (See family record on page 106).

XXX.—(8) Jacob Hole, born July 18th, 1828, is the last surviving child of Charles Hole and Esther Hanna. He married, Oct. 24th, 1867, Amelia Morlan, daughter of Mordecai and Elizabeth (Dean) Morlan, a sister to Caroline, wife of Robert Hole, his brother. Jacob Hole has been for many years a merchant and furniture dealer in Salem, Ohio, where he now resides. Jacob and Amelia Hole have issue,

XXXI.—(1) Dr. Charles M. Hole, (See portrait and sketch,) born Aug. 11th, 1868, married Carrie McArtor, physician, Cleveland, Ohio.

XXXI.—(2) Edgar T. Hole, (See portrait and sketch) born Nov. 28th, 1869, married Adalaide M. Weider, Apr. 14th, 1897 and had issue,

    (1) Margaret, died in infancy.

    (2) Leona M., born Jan 17th, 1902. Edgar T. Hole with his wife and daughter, Leona M. are in Africa, as missionaries of the Friend's church and stationed at Kesumu, British East Africa.

XXXI.—(3) Wilmer Dean, born Apr. 1st, 1872, married Susie Lavina Jones, June 29th, 1901 and resides in California.

XXXI.—(4) Virginia L., born Sept. 13th, 1873, married Dr. Elisha Blackburn, and in May, 1903 went with him to British East Africa, where they are sent by the Friend's Church, as missionaries.

XXXI.—(5) Esther Eliza, born Jan. 26th, 1875, married Addison Fritchman, born Aug. 4th, 1897, and died May 13, 1902, leaving issue,

    (1) Eleanor Fritchman, born June 28th, 1898.

    (2) Stephen Fritchman, born May 12th, 1902.

XXXI.—(6) J. Leroy Hole, born July 14th, 1876.

XXXI.—(7) Harry R. Hole, born Aug, 20th, 1881.

XXX.—(9) "Aunt Hannah," ninth child of Charles and Esther Hole, never married. She lived for others and was beloved by her brothers and sisters families and by all who knew her. She died on the fifty-fifth anniversary of her birth, April 10th, 1887, while on a visit to her brother, in Jennings County, Indiana.

Charles Morlan Hole was born at Salem, Ohio, August 11, 1868. He attended the public schools of his native city. and afterwards entered the employ of the Buckeye Engine Company, of Salem, and became an expert mechanical engineer, and for several years supervised the erection and installation of the engines manufactured by this famous company.

He then entered the medical department of Western Reserve University at Cleveland, Ohio, from which he graduated in 1898. By securing the highest ranks at a competitive examination, he won the appointment as resident physician of the Cleveland City Hospital, and served as such until January 1, 1900, when he went into general practice at No. 300 Cedar avenue, Cleveland, where he still resides.

He was married to Miss Carrie McArtor, of Salem, Ohio, in November, 1900, and finds in her a real helpmate in his profession. He has been honored by the authorities of the Forest City by appointment to the offices of District Physician and Medical Inspector of the city, and is also acting as Medical Inspector of the Ohio State Board of Health.

He is a member of the clinical staff of Lakeside Hospital Dispensary, and is the Medical Examiner of the Western and Southern Life Insurance Company, of Cincinnati, Ohio.

He is over six feet in stature and tips the beam at more than two hundred pounds, and the brief vacations which he allows himself are generally spent in tramping over the hills of Columbiana County in company with his double cousin Judge Hole, at which times they drink copious draughts from the spring where their great grandfather Robert Hanna, built his first log-cabin one hundred years ago, and test their marksmanship with the rifle, which is their invariable companion. But which of these gentlemen is entitled to be called champion, either as pedestrian or marksman, the author of this book is unable to state. As each one fiercely claims that title after each annual outing, it would require a bolder and a larger man to safely decide the question. By way of post-scriptural advice, however, he would suggest that if these two contestants will journey to the wilds of Jennings County, Indiana, and follow for a single day in the footsteps of that peerless master of woodcraft, Charles Fremont Hole, of Butlerville, they will return to the Buckeye State thoroughly silenced and subdued.

Edgar T. Hole was born at Salem, Ohio, Nov. 28, 1869. After completing the grammar and high school courses, he spent several years in the study of architecture and draughting. While living in Cleveland in 1893, he gave up this work, temporarily, on account of his eyes, and took a business position which he held until 1902, when with two other young men he was sent by a board of the Society of Friends to prospect and establish a missionary station in Africa. Here his wife and child, with other missionaries joined him a year later. He was married to Adelaide Weider, of Cleveland in 1897. They have one daughter, Leona May, born Jan. 17, 1902.

During his residence of more than two years in Cleveland, he was active in business and church work. In his church he held the office of elder, overseer and treasurer; he was a Sabbath school teacher, C. E. president, trustee of the Friends' Bible Institute, and gave much time and energy to local mission work. He is at present superintendent and treasurer of the Friends' Africa Industrial Missions at Kaimosi, Tiriki, British East Africa. (This is in the Kaviroudo Country, about 20 miles from Kisumu, the principal port on Lake Victoria Nyanza; about 8 miles north of the equator and at an elevation of about 5300 feet above sea level.)

CHAPTER XIV.

DESCENDANTS OF JOHN HOLE AND CATHARINE HANNA.

29TH GENERATION.—(2) John Hole, born in Loudoun County, Va., Jan. 7, 1785, removed to Ohio in 1816. Raised in Bedford County, Va., in the southern part of that state, he was familiar with the southern country and was employed, during the war of 1812 by the U. S. Government, in hauling supplies from North and South Carolina to Baltimore and Philadelphia. After completing his contract as "wagouer" for the government he returned to Bedford County, Va., and while working on his father's farm taught "singing school." This is the first instance known of any musical ability in the Hole family. In 1817, at Carmel (Clarkson, O.,) he became engaged to Catharine Hanna, and as a specimen of the *modus operandi* of the Society of Friends at that period, the following extracts from the records of Carmel meeting will be valuable. "Agreeably to the directions of the quarterly meeting, the monthly meeting was opened at Carmel the 20th of the 12th month, 1817. At this meeting, John Hole and Catharine Hanna appear here with parents' consent and express their intentions of marriage with each other. Edith Marsh and Deborah Vale are appointed to inquire into the young woman's clearness of the like engagement with others and report to next meeting."

"17th of 1st month, 1818—The friends appointed to enquire into Catharine Hanna's clearness with respect to marriage engagement report they find nothing to obstruct. They are left at liberty to accomplish the same agreeably to good order. Edith Marsh and Deborah Vale are appointed to attend and see that moderation be observed and report to next meeting."

"Twenty-first of 2nd month, 1818." The friends appointed to attend the marriage of John Hole and Catharine Hanna, report they thought it orderly accomplished and moderation observed." The certificate reads as follows: "Whereas John Hole of Middleton Township, Columbiana County and State of Ohio, son of Jacob Hole of the same County and Mary his wife; and Catharine Hanna, daughter of Robert Hanna and Catharine his wife, of Middleton Township, Columbiana County, Ohio, having declared their intentions of marriage with each other before a Monthly Meeting of the religious Society

of Friends, held at Carmel according to the good order used among them, and having consent of parents, their said proposal of marriage was allowed by said meeting. Now these are to certify whom it may concern that for the full accomplishment of their said intentions this twenty-second day of the first mouth in the year of our Lord, one thousand eight hundred and eighteen, they, the said John Hole and Catharine Hanna, appeared in a publick meeting of the said people held at Carmel, and the said John Hole taking the said Catharine Hanna by the hand did openly declare that he took her, the said Catharine Hanna, to be his wife, promising with divine assistance, to be unto her a loving and faithful husband until death should separate them, and then in the same assembly the said Catharine Hanna, did in like manner declare that she took him, the said John Hole to be her husband, promising with divine assistance to be unto him a loving and faithful wife until death should separate them. And more-over they, the said John Hole and Catharine Hanna (she according to the custom of marriage assuming the name of her husband) did as a further confirmation thereof, then and there to these presents set their hands.   JOHN HOLE,
                                 CATHARINE HOLE.

And we whose names are hereunto subscribed being present at the solemnization of the said marriage and subscription, have as witnesses thereto set our hands the day and year above written."

Willin Underwood,	Robert Hanna,
Sarah Underwood,	Catharine Hanna,
Rebecca Underwood,	Nathan Hole.
Rachel Fisher, Jr.,	Mary Morlan,
Susannah Heacock,	Sophia Hole,
Sarah Heacock,	Nathan Hole, Jr.,
Elizabeth West,	Jonah Hole,
Eli Vale,	Thos. Hannah,
Wm. Fisher,	Anne Hanna,
Charles Hambleton,	Joshua Hanna.
William Griffith,	Benj'n Hambleton,
Willin Underwood, Jr.	Mahlon Hole,
Ephraim Oliphant,	Benj'n Hanna,
Jane McMillen,	Jane Leech,
Thomas Green,	William Leech,
Elie Edmundson,	Deborah Vale,
Jason Tulloss,	James Marsh,
Jonathan Marsh,	Edith Marsh,
Elizabeth Hole,	John Vale.
Elizabeth Dillon.	

"Recorded in Carmel's records for Marriage certificates; Page 5."

John and Catharine Hole began housekeeping on "Muddy Fork," in the Eastern part of Carroll County, and at this home and one adjoining, where they soon after settled, were born to them eight children. John Hole was a man of great business ability and had the care and settlement of many estates. He was for several terms one of Carroll Counties' Commissioners and associated with the Hon. Ephraim R. Eckley, who still survives at the age of 93 years. His death occurred quite suddenly, in his 84th year, soon after he had walked from his home to Minerva and back, a distance of ten miles. Catharine Hole survived her husband for many years. She was an Elder in Augusta Friends' Meeting for more than 50 years. For the last seven years of her life she was partially paralyzed. She died May 3rd, 1881 aged 87 years and was the last of her generation of the Hanna family. Both John and Catharine Hole were buried at the Augusta Friends' Meeting House, where are interred some forty members of the Hole and Hanna families.

THE CHILDREN OF JOHN AND CATHARINE HOLE.

XXX.—(1) Lemuel Hole, born Oct. 27, 1818, died Jan. 20, 1865.

(2) Elias Hole, born May 4, 1820, died Oct. 22, 1873.

(3) Esther Hole, born May 7, 1822, died Aug. 18, 1890.

(4) Anna Hole, born June 15, 1824, died Nov. 2, 1850.

(5) Caleb Hole, born March 6, 1827, Damascus, Ohio.

(6) Robert H. Hole, born June 16, 1829, died Dec. 5, 1866.

(7) Mary Hole, born April 2, 1833, died July 9, 1839.

(8) Rachel Hole, born Aug. 16, 1837, Alliance, Ohio.

(1) Lemuel Hole was married to Unity C. Stanley, Apr. 30th, 1840. She was the daughter of Benjamin and Elizabeth Stanley, born Jan, 27th, 1820, died Aug. 29th, 1885. Lemuel Hole was a most honorable, honest and upright man; a man of great business ability and of a good mind. He was associated with the leaders and organizers of the Republican party and corresponded with such men as Joshua R. Giddings, Benjamin F. Wade and S. P. Chase. He died at the early age of forty-seven years, Jan. 20th, 1865, having amassed what at that day was considered a handsome fortune. Lemuel and Unity Hole were both buried at the Augusta Friend's meeting house.

CHILDREN OF LEMUEL AND UNITY HOLE.

XXXI.—(1) Benjamin Stanley, born Apr. 12th, 1841, resides in Alliance, Ohio.

(2) Gulaelma, born Nov. 26th, 1842, died June 18th, 1856.

(3) Leonard Hannah, born June 23rd, 1844, 59 Cedar Street, N. Y. City.

[4] Catharine Elizabeth, born Oct. 5th, 1846, Damascus, Ohio.

[5] Eliza Anna, born Dec. 27th, 1848, Lawrence, Kansas.

[6] John Franklin, born Mar. 19th, 1852, died Dec. 17th, 1856.

[7] Jacob Thomas, Mar. 18th, 1854, died in Kansas, 1896.

[8] Charles Stanley, born Aug. 11th, 1856, living in Texas.

[9] Esther Elma, born July 31st, 1858, Millersburg, Ohio.

[10] Lemuel Penrose, born Nov. 5th, 1860, Spokane, Washington.

XXXI.—(1) Benjamin Stanley Hole, married, March 10, 1868, Mary Marshall and had issue,

XXXII.—(1) Rosella C. Hole, born Dec. 17, 1868, married, Oct. 10, 1889, Clifton Cunningham (born Feb. 19, 1867), resides at Sebring, O., and has Owen L., born Jan. 29, 1891 and Paul C., born May 29, 1892.

XXXII.—(2) Lavina U., born Jan. 1, 1870; married Dec. 25, 1894, James Wooster Ogle* and has issue,

(1) Marshall Rodney Ogle, born Oct. 3, 1895.

(2) Mary Ruth Ogle, born Sept. 27, 1897.

(3) Carl Henry Ogle, born Jan. 5, 1900.

XXXII.—(3) Linneus M., born June 1, 1871, married Anna L. Roach born March 27, 1874, and has issue,

(1) Franklin H. Hole, born June 10, 1893.

(2) Arthur J. Hole, born April 7, 1900.

XXXII.—(4) Lemuel G. Hole, born April, 7, 1881, married Mary E. Betts (born Sept. 16, 1879), Oct. 27, 1900.

Benjamin Stanley Hole married (2nd) Mrs. Eliza J. Abel, of Kilgore, Ohio, and now resides on Rice street, Alliance, Ohio.

XXXI.—(3) Leonard Hanna Hole married Sarah Belle Moffatt, of Cadiz, Ohio, July 13, 1870 (daughter of John N. Moffatt and Margaret Jane Ramsey, daughter of John L. Ramsey and Sarah Ann Slaytor,) and had issue,

---

*James Wooster Ogle, is a great-grand-nephew of Caesar Rodney, a signer of the Declaration of Independence; and a cousin to the Caesar A Rodney, who was Attorney General of the United States. On the maternal side, James W. Ogle is a great-grandnephew of General Wooster of Revolutionary fame. He was born April 19, 1852, and resides at 418 Kirtland Ave., Cleveland, Ohio.

XXXII.—(1) Jay Wilberforce, born April 13, 1871; died at Las Crucus, N. Mexico, Feb. 2, 1892.

(2) Lemuel Homer, born December 4, 1874.

(3) Charles Benjamin, born Feb. 22, 1878.

(4) Ralph John, born June 26, 1884.

Charles Benjamin Hole (32-3) married June 20, 1901, Nina May Howlett, daughter of T. A. and Adelia A. Howlett, of Ann Arbor, Michigan.

Of this family Leonard Hanna Hole and his wife, Belle Moffatt, were students of Mt. Union College. Leonard H., graduated in the class of 1868. Lemuel Homer Hole graduated in the class of 1899 from the University of Michigan, Law Department. Chas. Benjamin Hole graducted in Law Department, University of Michigan, 1899, and his wife, Nina May Howlett, in the the Literary Course, University of Michigan, 1901.

LEONARD HANNA HOLE, who is now associated with the firm of W. N. Coler & Co., Bankers and Brokers, of New York City, has been an eminently successful business man and lawyer ever since his gradution from Mount Union College in 1868. Previous to entering college he had seen military service in the Civil War, and after its close had remained in the South, during a part of the reconstruction period, teaching in south-eastern Virginia and establishing schools amongst the ex-slaves in and about Yorktown and Norfolk.

After graduation he studied law and practiced in Iowa, Kansas and Dakota. He was a member of the State Constitutional Convention of South Dakota and controlled that body so completely that he was the first choice of the people for Governor of the State. He had such extensive business interests, however, at this time, that he refused the position as he had done previously in another western state. He has always refused to hold office though many have been offered and almost thrust upon him. He has been extensively engaged in large business firms and has successfully carried his company through financial panics when hundreds of the companies have failed. He has been something of a lobbyist and has been frequently sent to Washington to advance Bills pending in Congress. He was the warm personal friend of President McKinley and equally of his cousin, Senator Marcus A. Hanna for whose father (Dr. Leonard Hanna) he was named. He is a member of the Lawyers' Club of New York City and a partner of Hon. Bird S. Coler, late City Comptroller of New York, and Democratic Candidate for Governor of New York State in 1902. For some years past he has resided in Flushing, a part of greater New York, but has recently built a home at Montclair, N. J., on the highest elevation in that region, a most commanding position, overlooking some eight or ten villages and cities and in full view of the long range of lights in New York City from Staten Island to Harlem. Leonard Hanna Hole visited his relative Dean Hole, of Rochester, England, some six years ago, and was so interested in the family history that he commissioned the present writer to go to England and obtain from the Dean and others the correct Hole genealogy. It is due, therefore, to this member of the family, that the "Hole Family History" is published. Had it not been for his generosity and assistance it would probably never have appeared in print.

XXXI.—(4th) Catharine Elizabeth Hole, married, July 14, 1870, Geo. Morton Bashaw (born Oct. 28, 1838, died Feb. 12, 1894) and had issue,

XXXII.—(1st) Lemuel Rolla, born May 21, 1871, married Clara Allison, Oct. 19, 1895, and has Walter Leonard, born Apr. 1, 1897, and Hazel Catharine, born Dec. 26, 1898.

(2nd) Ottiwell Wilfred, born May 3rd, 1873, married Effie Evilin Stutler, Oct. 23, 1897, and has, Lucile Genevera, born Oct. 19, 1902.

(3rd) John Herbert, born Aug. 16, 1881, married Aug. 20, 1902, Gertrude May Griffeth.

(4th) Clyde Leonard Bashaw, born Aug. 2nd, 1887.

XXXI.—(5th) Eliza Anna Hole, married Robert Terrell Crew, of Jefferson Co., Ohio, (Aug. 12, 1846) married Mar. 4, 1869. Resides in Lawrence, Kansas, and has issue,

XXXII.—(1st) Elizabeth Crew, Jan. 16, 1870, married Arthur E. Huddleston, of Douglas Co, Kansas, (born Nov. 30, 1860) Nov. 17, 1902, has issue a daughter, (name not given.)

(2nd) Chas. Corwin Crew, born in Iowa, Dec. 17, 1871, married Grace Lena Cross [born June 29, 1876] Jan. 1, 1902.

[3rd] Mary Catherine Crew, born in Iowa, Oct. 15, 1875, an artist, studied in Italy and in New York City 1900–1903.

XXXI.—[7] Jacob Thomas Hole, married Mary Emma Tope, June 10th, 1880. He was a graduate of Mt. Union College, class 1878, and of Penn College, Iowa; practiced law and was an Editor in Washington, Kansas, where he died in 1896. Jacob and Emma Hole had issue,

XXXII.—[1] Lemuel Everett,

[2] Gertrude Elma,

[3] William Warren,

[4] Leonard Lamar,

[5] Clarence Frederick,

[6] Walter Tope,

[7] Esther Grace,

[8] A younger daughter, name not given.

XXXI.—[8] Charles Stanley Hole, married Hannah W. Young, [born Jan. 16th, 1860], on Apr. 14th, 1880 and has issue.

XXXII.—[1] Edward Lemuel, born Mar. 5th, 1881.*

[2] Carl Clifford, born July 3rd, 1884.

[3] Elizabeth, born Oct. 17th, 1889, died Dec. 22nd, 1902.

[4] Esther, born Oct. 20th, 1894.

[5] William T., born May 31st, 1896.

XXXI.—(9) Esther Elma Hole, married Hon. John Anderson Mc-Dowell (born Sept. 25, 1853), Aug. 21, 1879. Resides at Millersburg, Ohio. Esther Elma Hole attended Mt. Union College, and was a member of the class of 1880. Her husband, born in Holmes Co., Ohio, was educated at Lebanon Normal University and Mt. Union College (class 1887), was Superintendent of the Millersburg schools for 17 years, County Examiner 7 years, instructor in Wooster University and various summer schools and institutes. Was elected to 55th Congress as a Democrat, receiving 26,109 votes, against 21,169 for Addison S. McClure, Republican; was re-elected to the 56th Congress. Since the expiration of his second term he has taught in Wooster University. To Mr. and Mrs. McDowell have been born twelve children:

XXXII.—James Garfield, born July 4, 1881; died Dec. 23, 1882.

[2] Waldo Emerson, born Dec. 1, 1882.

[3] Clyde Stanley, born Oct. 28, 1884.

[4] Edith Bell, born Jan. 23, 1887.

[5] Homer Hole, born Aug. 20, 1889.

[6] Mabel Margaret, Aug. 4, 1891.

[7] Percy Hanna, July 8, 1893.

[8] Frances Willard, Oct. 21, 1895.

[9] John Anderson, July 3, 1897.

[10] Wilbur Hutchinson, } Twins { born Nov. 21, 1898; died Dec. 12, 1898.

[11] Wayne Allison, } { born Nov. 21, 1898.

[12] Esther Aimee, born Feb. 4, 1901, died Aug. 9, 1902.

---

*Edward Lemuel Hole enlisted in the Regular Army, Company G, 18th Infantry and served three years as a private; over two years of the time in the Phillipine Islands.

one of the chief heads of the Ohio Yearly Meeting of Friends he has held various offices of trust and has brought to a successful termination much of the committee work and handled large amounts of the meeting's trust funds. From these arduous duties he has now, at his own request, been released, with regret on the part of the Yearly Meeting. He was known as the bachelor of the family as he remained at home with his parents, but during his bachelor days he cared for and raised the two sons of his brother Robert, who are now successful business men and farmers and both of them eminently christian gentlemen; a credit to the uncle who raised them and to the entire family. After the death of his father in 1868, Caleb Hole married Sophia Miller, widow of his cousin Jacob G. Hole [See Miller family appendix]. To them were born a son and a daughter. The son Dr. Norman W. Hole, was educated at Damascus Academy, Mt. Union College and the Western Reserve Medical College. Graduating with the degree of M. D., in 1898 from the Wooster Medical College, Cleveland, Ohio, he afterwards took post-graduate work, [Hospital and Clinic] in New York City. Dr. N. W. Hole married Lena Cobbs, a grand-daughter of an eminent minister in the Disciple Church, the Rev. John Schaeffer, who is still living and in splendid health, in his ninety-ninth year. Dr. Hole is the father of three children, Donald, Bertha and Alfred, and successfully practices his profession in North Jackson, Ohio.

The daughter, Anna Lula Hole, one of the most intellectual members of the Hole family, died in Cleveland, Ohio, Feb. 8, 1896, at the early age of 22 years. She was educated at Damascus Academy, Earlham College, Indiana, and graduated in the Classical Course from Mt. Union College, in 1893, being the youngest member of her class. While in college she belonged to the Delta Gamma Sorority and was an active worker in the Republican Literary Society. She was engaged as teacher of Modern Languages in Jefferson Institute, Jefferson, Ohio, and afterwards taught in Andover, Ohio, and in Collinwood, Ohio.

XXX.—(6) Robert H. Hole, born May 16, 1899, married Lydia H. Lipsey, Oct. 27, 1853, died in Logansport, Indiana, Dec. 5, 1865. Lydia Hole died May 31, 1889, leaving issue.

XXXI.—(1) Leander H. Hole, born Dec. 6, 1854, married Ida Coulson (Oct. 17, 1857), Jan. 16, 1879, Merchant at Lupton, Michigan, and has issue one son, Erwin Jay Hole, born Oct. 14, 1883.

(2) J. Melville Hole, born April 27, 1859, married Lovisa E. Haldeman (June 22, 1861), Dec., 1882, daughter of David and Julia (Eastman) Haldeman. (See David Haldeman, above in

Anna Hole XXX (4)). J. Melville and Lovisa E. Hole have one daughter, Gertrude F. Hole. They reside near Kensington, Ohio.

XXX.—(7) Mary Hole, born April 2, 1833, married Henry Tritt. She died July 6, 1850, leaving issue, 1. Edward Tritt and 2. Charles Tritt. Edward Tritt married and resides in Cripple Creek, Colorado, has five children. Charles Tritt died in Alliance, Ohio, without issue.

XXX.—(8) Rachel Hole, eighth child of John Hole and Catharine (Hanna) Hole, married, Dec. 29, 1858, Dr. William Pettit Rice, only son of Charles Hawley Rice and Charity Dean Pettit (see "Pettit Family Geneaolgy," by Charles E. Rice). They removed to Stearns County, Minnesota, where, being on the frontier, they suffered many hardships and had thrilling experiences with the Sioux and Chippewa Indians. William P. Rice was County Surveyor of Stearns Co., and did government work at Fort Snelling during the Indian outbreaks and the Civil War. Returning to Ohio they settled in Mt. Union [now Alliance], where Dr. Rice practiced dentistry until his death, Dec. 9, 1891. He was for several terms mayor of the city, president and clerk of the school board, 18 years a councilman and 22 years a steward and treasurer of the M. E. Church, in which latter position he was succeeded by his oldest son who has been treasurer and steward in the Union Ave., M. E. Church for 15 years. He was a graduate of Duff's College, and a good business man, occupying positions of trust from the time he was seventeen years of age till his death.

Rachel Hole Rice, now residing at 1750 South Union Avenue, Alliance, Ohio, is an active worker in reform movements, having held various offices in the State, County and Local W. C. T. U., Woman's Suffrage Association, Woman's Foreign Missionary Society of the M. E. Church, etc., etc. To W. P. and R. H. Rice were born seven children:

XXXI.—[1st] Ida May Rice, married Joseph A. Wright, Oct. 22. 1896, and resides at 131 Pigeon St, Jackson, Michigan.

[2nd] Charles Elmer Rice, 1750 S. Union Ave., Alliance, O.

[3rd] William Oscar Rice, died in infancy.

[4th] John Clarence Rice, married Pearl Frances Grubb,* Sept. 17, 1896 and has issue,

[1st] William Elmer Rice.

*See "Grubb of Horsenden," Appendix.

[2nd] Joseph Clarence Rice.

[3rd] Verda Mae Rice.

All residing on Rice Street, Alliauce, Ohio.

XXXI.—[5th] Robert Emerson Rice, died in infancy.

[6th] Virginia Alpharetta Rice, married Herman Norville Morton, † Dec. 24, 1897 and has issue one son,

XXXII.—Charles Theodore Morton, born in Sandusky, Ohio, where his father was Principal of the High School. Prof. Morton is at present Principal of the Urbana, Ohio, High School; address 407 East Church Street, Urbana, Ohio.

XXXI.—(7) William Herbert Rice married Dec. 25, 1901, Mina Mae Miller (see Miller family, appendix.) He is a graduate of Mt. Union College, with degree of Mus. B., and has been a student of the Metropolitan College of Music, N. Y. City, studying under such celebrated musicians and composers as Harry Rowe Shelley, Prof. Albert Ross Parsons, H. Rawlins Baker and William Sherman. His present address is 170 Amity street, Flushing, New York City, where he is engaged in teaching music A portrait is here given of William Herbert Rice, who is the youngest child of the youngest child of John and Catharine Hole.

†See 'Morton Family," Appendix.

In Memoriam.

To

**Charlotte, daughter of Abi Hole and Peter Preston;
Esther, daughter of John and Catharine Hole;
Hannah, daughter of Charles and Esther Hole;
Mary, daughter of Mahlon and Rachel Hole.**

Blessed are the Aunt Marys and Aunt Hannahs, the Aunt Charlottes and the Aunt Esthers of the Hole family! Having no children of their own they lived lives of devotion to their nephews and neices. To us they were the loves of our childhood and the admiration of our maturer years. Often, in toil and pain, they ministered to us and we showed little appreciation. Their monuments will not make much show in the churchyard. Their names will not be passed down to posterity with many wreaths about them. But they are God's favorites. Their work is blessed. In this world they were like modest, lowly flowers, hidden away but pouring out sweet perfumes and filling the air with their odors. And in heaven they will get their reward, not praise of men, but open confession by the Lord himself and 'other people's children shall rise up and call them blessed.'

APPENDIX A.

The Hannas were ancestors of the hundreds of descendants of Charles Hole and John Hole [Generation XXIX.] who married the sisters, Esther and Catharine Hanna. Robert Hanna, father of Esther and Catharine Hole, came to America with his father Thomas Hanna, when but ten years old. This was in the year 1763, and we find that there was, long before that date, a Scotch-Irish family of Hannas settled in Pennsylvania. The two families must not be confused. Thomas Hanna and his family, consisting of six children, with the mother Elizabeth [Henderson] Hanna, settled in Chester County, Pa., but afterwards removed to Lynchburg, Virginia, where he died in 1801 and she in 1800. They came to America from County Monahan, Ireland, where the six children were born, viz:

[1] John Hanna, born in 1749. Died at Newcastle on the Tyne, on shipboard, in 1763, aged 13 years.

[2] James Hanna, born March 2nd, 1753.

[3] Robert Hanna, born March 2nd, 1753. [a twin.]

[4] Hugh Hanna, born 1755.

[5] Martha Hanna, (Saunders) Jan. 1st, 1758.

[6] Thomas Hanna, born 1760.

Of the above named six children of Thomas Hanna, James, [2] was twice married and had a family of thirteen children. Hugh, [4] married and had a family of eight children. [5] Martha married a Saunders and left, in Virginia, posterity traced in the Hanna Book. [6] Thomas married and had a family of six children. [3] ROBERT HANNA, our ancestor, married, in Chester County, Pa., Catharine Jones, on Jan. 31st, 1776. Catharine Jones was born Aug. 27th, 1754, and died in Lisbon, Ohio, Sept. 28th, 1835, in her 82nd year. Robert and Catharine Hanna settled in the Battle Field of the Brandywine and there their oldest son, Thomas, was born, May 2nd, 1777. In 1779 they removed to the southern part of Virginia where Robert Hanna, in partnership with John Lynch, laid out the city of Lynchburg on lands owned by them. The city took the name of Lynch from the Senior Proprietor, although Robert Hanna had an almost equal ownership. At Lynchburg eight children were born to Robert and Catharine Hanna, between the years 1779 and 1797, and in 1801 they removed from Campbell County, Va., and settled in the eastern part of Columbiana County, [at that time Jefferson County] in the present state of Ohio. Here the tenth child, Joshua, was born.

Robert Hanna died July 17th, 1837 at the home of his daughter Catharine Hole, near Augusta, Ohio, and was buried at Augusta Friends' Meeting House. It is not the intention to give here an extended or complete history of the Hanna family. This will be found in another volume.

THE CHILDREN OF ROBERT AND CATHARINE HANNA.

[1] Thomas, born May 2, 1777; died Sept. 17, 1828, in Lisbon, O.

[2] Benjamin, born June 14, 1779; died 1849 in Lisbon, O.

[3] Esther [1st], born Aug. 6, 1871; died Nov. 3, 1791, buried in South River graveyard, Lynchburg.

[4] David, born Jan. 9, 1784; died Oct. 24, 1791, buried in South River graveyard, Lynchburg.

[5] Caleb, born Sept. 4, 1786; died July 15, 1790, buried in South River graveyard, Lynchburg.

[6] Robert, born June 20, 1789; died Sept. 25, 1854 at Wilmington, Delaware.

[7] Esther [2nd], born April 10, 1792; died Dec. 6, 1849, at Carmel, Columbiana Co., Ohio.

[8] Catharine, born Nov. 25, 1794; died May 3, 1881, Augusta, Ohio.

[9] Ann, born July 30, 1797, died March 3, 1867 in Iowa.

[10] Joshua, born Feb. 16, 1802; died Sept. 11, 1804, Middleton, O.
Of the five children who married and left descendants:

[2] Benjamin married Rachel Dixon and had eleven children, seven boys and four girls. One of these sons, Dr. Leonard Hanna, was the father of the Hon. Marcus Alonzo Hanna, United States Senator from Ohio, who was born Sept. 24, 1837, in Lisbon, Ohio.

[6] Robert Hanna married Elizabeth Liston, and left a family of two sons and three daughters. He was a portrait painter. He painted in the south for many years, and died in Wilmington, Delaware. He was also ordained a Methodist minister by Bishop Asbury, but did not remain long in the ministry.

[7] Esther Hanna married Charles Hole. She was a minister in the Society of Friends. Died in Columbiana Co., Ohio, Dec. 6, 1849. Her descendants are given in the closing chapters of this book.

(8) Catharine Hanna married John Hole. She lived in Carroll and Columbiana Counties [Ohio], from 1801 to 1881, dying in Carroll County, near Augusta, May 3, 1881, aged 87 years. A complete list of her descendants will be found in the closing chapters of this volume.

(9) Ann Hanna married Benjamin Hambleton, raised a family of seven children, removed to Iowa and died there in 1867.

APPENDIX B.

SIR ANDREW DOUGLAS (1248) younger son of Sir Archibald, the second chief of the house of Douglas, was father of

WILLIAM DOUGLAS, who in 1296 swore fealty to Edward I, for his lands in West Lothian, whose son, by Elizabeth, daughter of Alexander, 4th High Steward.

JAMES DOUGLAS, of Lothian, in 1315, had a grant from Robert I. He died 1320, having had Sir William and Sir John.

SIR WILLIAM DOUGLAS, of Liddesdale, the elder son, acquired the lordship of Dalkeith (an old possession of the Grahams), the Barony of Aberdour, in Fife, lands in Tweeddale and great territories in Liddesdale, Eskdale and Ewesdale, which had been forfeited by the Soulises and the Lovels. He met his death in 1353 at the hands of the first Earl of Douglas. He had no male issue and in 1351 entailed his property on the 5 sons of his brother John.

SIR JOHN DOUGLAS, younger brother of the Knight of Liddesdale, had by his wife Agnes Monfode, with other issue, 1st, James (Sir), of Dalkeith and Sir Henry, of Lugton and Lochlevan, who married Marjory [died 1438] daughter of Sir John Stewart, a half brother of King Robert II. Had a long line of descendants. Sir John Douglas was assassinated by order of Sir David Barclay in 1350, and Barclay was slain by his brother, Sir William Douglas.

SIR JAMES DOUGLAS, of Dalkeith, eldest son of above, succeeded in 1353 to the possessions of his uncle William Douglas. He was distinguished for his learning and accomplishments. He married in 1371, Agnes of Dunbar, daughter of Patrick, Earl of March. He died in 1420, having issue, James, his successor, William, John and Jacoba, who married Sir James Hamilton, of Cadzon.

SIR JAMES DOUGLAS, of Dalkeith, had in 1401 a charter of the Barony of Morton, in Nithsdale. He married Lady Elizabeth, daughter of King Robert III, by whom he had William, James, his father's heir, and Henry. By second marriage had Sir William of Morton and Whittingham.

SIR JAMES DOUGLAS, second Lord of Dalkeith, married Elizabeth daughter of Gifford of Sheriffhall and had issue, a daughter Beatrix, married to first Earl of Erroll, and a son.

JAMES DOUGLAS, third Lord Dalkeith, who was made EARL OF MORTON, on his marriage with the Princess Johanna, daughter of James I, of Scotland, in March, 1457. Had issue,

JAMES, SECOND EARL OF MORTON, who succeeded his father in 1504, and had issue,

JAMES, THIRD EARL OF MORTON, married Katherine, daughter of James IV and had daughters, Margaret, Beatrix, and Elizabeth. On April 23d, 1543 the third Earl executed a conveyance of his Earldom to his youngest daughter's husband (James Douglas, second son of Sir George Douglas), who became

JAMES, FOURTH EARL OF MORTON, succeeded his father-in-law in 1553. He was chancellor under Queen Mary and Regent of Scotland from 1572-1578. He was executed in June 1581 and the Earldom passed to the son of the third Earl's second daughter, Lord Maxwell.

LORD MAXWELL was deposed and Archibald Douglas became, by act of James (Maxwell being accounted sixth Earl.)

ARCHIBALD, SEVENTH EARL OF MORTON, who was succeeded by

SIR WILLIAM DOUGLAS OF LOCHLEVAN, who left a large family but was succeeded by his grandson,

WILLIAM, 9TH EARL OF MORTON, K. G. and Lord High Treasurer of Scotland. By Royal Charter the islands of Orkney and Zetland were granted to him June 15, 1643. He married Lady Anne Keith, by whom he had a large family, two of his sons succeeding him, (as 10th and 12th Earls) He died in Orkney, Aug. 7th, 1648.

ROBERT DOUGLAS, 10TH EARL OF MORTON, married Elizabeth, daughter of Sir Edward Villiers, by whom he had issue,

WILLIAM DOUGLAS, 11TH EARL OF MORTON, who procured a new grant of the islands of Orkney and Zetland, but these lands were annexed by the Crown Dec. 27th, 1669. He married Lady Grizel Middleton, daughter of John, 1st Earl of Middleton, but died without surviving issue in 1681 and the Earldom reverted to his uncle,

JAMES DOUGLAS, 12TH EARL OF MORTON, who married Anne, daughter of Sir John Hay, and had issue,

JAMES DOUGLAS, 13TH EARL and his brother,

ROBERT DOUGLAS, 14TH EARL, who died unmarried and was succeeded by his brother.

GEORGE DOUGLAS, 15TH EARL, a Lieut. Col., in the Army and M. P. for Orkney prior to his inheritance. He married, (1st) a daughter of Muirhead of Linhouse, Edinburg. Married (2nd) Frances, daughter of William Adderly, of Halstow, in Kent, by whom he had,

JAMES 16TH, EARL, born 1703, married (1) Agatha, daughter of James Halliburton, by whom he had two surviving children, Sholto, Charles and Mary. Married (2nd) in 1755, Bridget, daughter of John Heathcote, Baronet, of Rutland, by whom he had another son and daughter whose descendants are mostly in the United States, and some of whom have been mentioned in the "Douglas-Thomas line" in this book. Mrs. Sarah Eleanor Douglas Holtz, now 92 years of age, whose portrait is shown, is the oldest known living descendant of the Douglas family of Morton. Her grandson, Prof. Herman Norville Morton, whose portrait is also given, is her oldest grandson and a great-great grandson of Thomas Thomas, the brother of Mary Thomas Hole whose portrait is given on page ——. Prof. Morton married Dec. 24, 1897, Virginia Alpharetta Rice, a great grandaughter of this Mary Thomas Hole.

APPENDIX C.

THE MILLER FAMILY.

There are recorded in this volume quite a number of inter-marriages between the Millers and the Holes. Several of the Millers have married into the Pennington family [3 brothers married 3 Pennington sisters.] We find Millers marrying into each generation of the Hole family from the 28th generation to the 32nd. It has been said of this family of Millers that they are like the measles, "when once they get started they go right through the family." Thus, Levi Miller [1774] married Ann Hole; his son, Robert, [1800-1895] married Catharine Hole, neice of Ann. Sophia Miller and Mary Miller, grand-daughters of Levi, married Jacob Hole and Israel Hole, [brothers] sons of Mahlon and Rachel Hole. Sophia married, 2nd, Caleb Hole, son of John and Catharine Hole. In the next generation Mina Mae Miller married William H. Rice, grandson of John Hole [1785-1868], etc., etc.

The first ancestor of this Miller family in the United States, was [1] Robert Miller who came from Ireland in 1745 and settled in Bucks County, Pa. Robert Miller married [1] Mary Shaw and had issue 9 children, [2] James, Mary, Robert, Jane, Samuel, Levi, Hannah and 2 other daughters.

[2] a   James married Mary Phillips, Bucks Co., Pa., issue 6 sons.

    b   Mary, married Nathan Walton.

    c   Robert, unmarried, a soldier and died in camp, 1812.

    d   Jane, married Jacob Hormal, had issue five children.

    e   Samuel, married, had one son and one daughter.

    f   Levi, born June 20, 1774 [noticed below].

    g   Hannah, married Thomas Ball.

    h   Two other sisters removed to Kentucky, married, but pos-terity not found.

[2] (f)   Levi Miller, son of Robert Miller and Mary Shaw, was born June 20, 1774, and died Aug. 6, 1838; married Deborah Morris in 1798 and had issue,

[3] a   Morris Miller, born July 27, 1799; died in 1884.

    b   Robert Miller, born Oct. 8, 1800; died Aug. 18, 1895.

c Isaac Miller, born March 24, 1802; died 1868.

d Nathan Miller, born Jan. 20, 1804; died March 20, 1808.

e Hannah Miller, born Sept. 28, 1805; died Oct. 1895.

f Mary Miller, born Feb. 23, 1807.

g Levi Miller, born Nov. 6, 1808.

h Sarah Miller, born Jan. 15, 1811.

i Samuel Miller, born Sept. 5, 1812; died in 1894.

j Rebecca Miller, born Oct. 9, 1814; died Sept. 18, 1895.

k Deborah Miller, born Oct. 22, 1816.

Levi Miller (3) g. married (3) Deborah Morris, oldest child of Isaac Morris and Hannah Perkins. She was born Sept. 9, 1777 and died Dec. 20, 1816. Her grandfather (1) Jonathan Morris of Chester County, Pa., came from Wales with the West family and married Mary West, an elder sister of Benjamin West, the famous artist and President of the Royal Academy of Fine Arts, (their little daughter, Sarah Morris, was the subject of Benjamin West's first drawing.) (2) Isaac Morris, son of Jonathan Morris and Mary West, born Jan. 31, 1751; (2) married Hannah Perkins who was born March 28, 1758, married 2nd, Elizabeth Lewis, born 28, April, 1767, and had issue,

(3) 1. Deborah, born Aug. 9, 1777, married (2) Levi Miller.

2. Sarah, born Aug. 1, 1779.

3. Benjamin, born Sept. 13, 1781.

4 and 5. Hannah and Isaac, born Nov. 17, 1782.

6. Mary, born Jan. 22, 1784.

7. Jonathan, born Apr. 7, 1787.

8. Phebe, born Nov. 17, 1789.

9. David, born Nov. 3, 1791.

SECOND WIFE'S CHILDREN.

10 Samuel, born Jan. 30, 1795.

11 Isaac, born 30th May, 1795.

12 Hannah, born 29th Dec., 1798.

13 Lewis, born 2nd April, 1800.

14 Mordecai, born 10th of November, 1801.

15 Rebecca, born 21st June, 1803.

16 Oliver C., born 25th July, 1805.

17 Elizabeth, born 21th May, 1807.

Out of the family of Isaac Morris, a grandson, Thomas C. Morris, [born 28th March, 1827] married Minerva J. Preston, [a daughter of Abi Hole and Peter Preston] born 27th of March, 1851; a granddaughter, Eliza Morris, married Caleb Preston, [son of Abi Hole and Peter Preston] 19th, of Nov. 1846. [See Preston family record.]

Another branch of the Miller family is found in West Moreland Co., Pa., descended from John Miller a nephew of Robert, [of Ireland [1]]

[1] John Miller was born in Dauphin Co., Pa., about 1765; had a son, [2] John, born in Dauphin Co., Pa., in 1792, who removed to Westmoreland Co., in 1815, and died in 1878, aged 86 years. John married [2] Sarah Deeds, of Mt. Pleasant, Pa., [1797-1877] daughter of [1] Abram Deeds. John and Sarah Miller were the parents of thirteen children, all now deceased but Rev. George B. Miller. [3] David D. Miller, born in Westmoreland Co., Pa., Jan. 19th, 1838, married [3] Sarah Smith, born July 12th, 1838. [3] Sarah Smith was the daughter of [2] Wm. Smith, of Latrobe [1800-1898] and [2] Elizabeth Rings [1801-1877] Wm. Smith [2] was son of John Smith [1] [1772-1807] and Catharine Shockey [1] [1773-1821]. His wife Elizabeth Rings Smith [2] was daughter of Michael Rings [1] and Catharine Rings [1]. The father of John Smith [1] came from Germany when very young, and settled in eastern Pa. This was Phillip Smith. [3] David D. Miller* and [3] Sarah Smith Miller had eight children:

1. Waldo Payson Miller.
2. Roberta Smith Roycroft, wife of E. M. Roycroft.
3. Raymond William Miller.
4. Milton Clarence Miller, died young.
5. Elsie Irene Eldredge, wife of Albert C. Eldridge.
6. Annette Wilson Miller.
7. Grace Elizabeth Miller.
8. Mina Mae Rice, wife of Wm. Herbert Rice.

---

* David D. Miller died Jan. 3rd, 1901, at Columbus, Ohio.

APPENDIX D.

PEDIGREE OF GRUBB OF HORSENDEN.

Taken from the Harleian manuscript 1547-99; Monumental Inscriptions; Parish Registers; Willis manuscript and other authorities.

(1) Henry Grubb of North Mimms, County Hertford, died 36th of Henry VIII(-1545) married Joan, daughter of Sir Richard Radcliffe, Knight, slain at Bosworth Field. The sister and heir of Sir John Radcliffe, knight; issue,

(2) George Grubb of North Mimms, who married Dorothy, daughter of Francis Clough, of Weston, County Hertford; issue,

[3] Eustace Grubb of North Mimms, died 1634. Married Constance daughter of —— Sheppard, of Hackley in March, 1581. Issue,

[4] John Grubb of Lincoln's Inn, born 1586. Married Mary, daughter of William Preston of Childwrick, March, 1612: Issue,

[5] John Grubb, born 1625, died June 16, 1700, buried 20 June, 1700 at Horsenden; Married Elizabeth, daughter of Henry Salmon of Cambridge, and widow of John Wilkinson; she died in 1700, aged 65 years: issue, Henry, James, EMANUEL and John.

[6] Emanuel Grubb born at Horsenden 25 June, 1679. Emigrated to America from Cornwall, England and settled on land in what is now Little Brittan Township, Lancaster County, Pa. Nearly 1000 acres of land were patented to him in that Township as early as 1713. There is a record of but one son,

[7] Thomas Grubb who inherited and lived on this land. Thomas Grubb's first wife was a McCreary, by whom he had three daughters: Ann, Charity and Prudence. His second wife was Isabella Polk. By this marriage he had seven sons: Joseph, Jacob, John, Thomas, James, William and Benjamin. The correct order may not be given, but we know that John Grubb was born June 8, 1767 and James Grubb in 1700. John Grubb (Captain), was sent to Erie County, Pennsylvania, in 1794 or '95, with a company of militia to guard the state surveyors. He remained in Erie County and took up lands there. His brother James accompanied him to Erie Co., and afterwards went into the Northwest Territory, settled at Chillicothe, Ross County, Ohio, and became one of the most useful citizens of the Territory. He was elected

a member of the Constitutional Convention of Ohio in 1802, and signed the State Constitution on Nov. 29, 1802. He never married, and died in Chillicothe, Ohio, 1805. In his father's will, probated in Erie County, Pa., in 1779 [when James was only 9 years old], he gives his son James "three hundred pounds, in current money of the State of Pennsylvania."

Joseph Grubb left a daughter [afterwards Mrs. Creigh] who was born in 1809 and died in 1893, aged 84 years. A grandson, Thomas A. Creigh, lives in Omaha, Neb. A grandson of Captain John Grubb, John G. Reed, lives at Millcreek, Pa.

[8] Jacob Grubb, son of Thomas, married Sarah Tettle, and had issue,

[9] Isaac Tettle Grubb, born 1802, died 1866, married Margaret McCurley, born 1804-1876 [daughter of John and Nancy Cornelius] had issue, ten children.

[10] a Susan Williamson, 1831, 1901.

   b John McCurley, 1833, 1858.

   c Nancy, 1836, 1869.

   d Anna L. Davis, 1839, Alliance, Ohio.

   e Mary Jane, 1841, 1842.

   f Isaac Jefferson, 1842, 1864.

   g Robert Marion, 1844, 1885.

   h Margaret Sarah [Mrs. Samuel Riddle] 1848, Enon, Pa.

   i Jasper Newton Grubb, 1851, Alliance, Ohio.

   j Jacob Allison Grubb, 1853, Oak Valley, Kansas.

   i Jasper Newton Grubb married Eliza Hoffman (daughter of

[3] Samuel Hoffman (1861-1901), and Sarah Bender. [3] Samuel was son of [2] Samuel and Fannie Hoffman, [2] Samuel was son of [1] Dietrict Hoffman). Had issue,

[1] Pearl Frances Grubb, born May 30, 1875; married, Sept. 17, 1896, John Clarence Rice, as in record of Rachel Hole Rice's family in this volume.

[2] Loyal Earnest Grubb, born April 29, 1877; married Dec. 25, 1901 to Rebecca Myers.

www.ingramcontent.com/pod-product-compliance
Lightning Source LLC
Chambersburg PA
CBHW070252290326
41930CB00041B/2465